Comptroller of the Currency
Administrator of National Banks

Loan Portfolio Management

Comptroller's Handbook

April 1998

A

Assets

Loan Portfolio Management

Table of Contents

Loan Portfolio
Management   Introduction

Overview

Lending is the principal business activity for most commercial banks. The loan portfolio is typically the largest asset and the predominate source of revenue. As such, it is one of the greatest sources of risk to a bank's safety and soundness. Whether due to lax credit standards, poor portfolio risk management, or weakness in the economy, loan portfolio problems have historically been the major cause of bank losses and failures.

Effective management of the loan portfolio and the credit function is fundamental to a bank's safety and soundness. Loan portfolio management (LPM) is the process by which risks that are inherent in the credit process are managed and controlled. Because review of the LPM process is so important, it is a primary supervisory activity. Assessing LPM involves evaluating the steps bank management takes to identify and control risk throughout the credit process. The assessment focuses on what management does to identify issues before they become problems. This booklet, written for the benefit of both examiners and bankers, discusses the elements of an effective LPM process. It emphasizes that the identification and management of risk among groups of loans may be at least as important as the risk inherent in individual loans.

For decades, good loan portfolio managers have concentrated most of their effort on prudently approving loans and carefully monitoring loan performance. Although these activities continue to be mainstays of loan portfolio management, analysis of past credit problems, such as those associated with oil and gas lending, agricultural lending, and commercial real estate lending in the 1980s, has made it clear that portfolio managers should do more. Traditional practices rely too much on trailing indicators of credit quality such as delinquency, nonaccrual, and risk rating trends. Banks have found that these indicators do not provide sufficient lead time for corrective action when there is a systemic increase in risk.

Effective loan portfolio management begins with oversight of the risk in individual loans. Prudent risk selection is vital to maintaining favorable loan quality. Therefore, the historical emphasis on controlling the quality of individual loan approvals and managing the performance of loans continues to be essential. But better technology and information systems have opened the door to better management methods. A portfolio manager can now obtain early indications of increasing risk by taking a more comprehensive view of the loan portfolio.

To manage their portfolios, bankers must understand not only the risk posed by each credit but also how the risks of individual loans and portfolios are interrelated. These interrelationships can multiply risk many times beyond what it would be if the risks were not related. Until recently, few banks used modern portfolio management concepts to control credit risk. Now, many banks view the loan portfolio in its segments and as a whole and consider the relationships among portfolio segments as well as among loans. These practices provide management with a more complete picture of the bank's credit risk profile and with more tools to analyze and control the risk.

In 1997, the OCC's Advisory Letter 97-3 encouraged banks to view risk management in terms of the entire loan portfolio. This letter identified nine elements that should be part of a loan portfolio management process. These elements complement such other fundamental credit risk management principles as sound underwriting, comprehensive financial analysis, adequate appraisal techniques and loan documentation practices, and sound internal controls. The nine elements are:

- Assessment of the credit culture,
- Portfolio objectives and risk tolerance limits,
- Management information systems,
- Portfolio segmentation and risk diversification objectives,
- Analysis of loans originated by other lenders,
- Aggregate policy and underwriting exception systems,
- Stress testing portfolios,
- Independent and effective control functions,
- Analysis of portfolio risk/reward tradeoffs.

Each of these elements is important to effective portfolio management. To a greater or lesser degree, each indicates the importance of the interrelationships among loans within the portfolio. Their focus is not on individual transactions, but on a group of similar transactions and on verifying the integrity of the process. Each practice, by itself, adds a dimension to loan portfolio management, but their value is amplified when they are used together; moreover, the absence of any one of these elements will diminish the effectiveness of the others. These elements are described in greater detail in appendix C and throughout the introductory section of this booklet.

All banks need to have basic loan portfolio management principles in place in some form. However, the need to formalize the various elements discussed in this booklet, and the sophistication of the process, will depend on the size of the bank, the complexity of its portfolio, and the types of credit risks it has assumed. For example, a community bank may be able to implement these principles in a less formal, less structured manner than a large bank and still have an effective loan portfolio management process. But even if the process is less formal, the risks to the loan portfolio discussed in this booklet should be addressed by all banks.

The examiner assigned LPM is responsible for determining whether the bank has an effective loan portfolio management process. This includes determining whether the risks associated with the bank's lending activities are accurately identified and appropriately communicated to senior management and the board of directors, and, when necessary, whether appropriate corrective action is taken.

This booklet contains important background information on loan portfolio management that examiners should review before conducting an asset quality examination. The risks unique to specific types of loans are addressed in several separate handbook booklets (e.g., "Commercial Real Estate and Construction Lending," "Lease Financing," and "Credit Card Lending").

Risks Associated with Lending

According to the OCC's supervision by risk philosophy, risk is the potential that events, expected or unexpected, may have an adverse impact on the bank's earnings or capital. The OCC has defined nine categories of risk for bank supervision purposes. These risks, which are defined in other Comptroller's Handbook sections, are credit, interest rate, liquidity, price, foreign exchange, transaction, compliance, strategic, and reputation. Banks with international operations are also subject to country risk and transfer risk. These risks are not mutually exclusive; any product or service may expose the bank to multiple risks. For analysis and discussion, however, the OCC identifies and assesses the risks separately.

A key challenge in managing risk is understanding the interrelationships of the nine risk factors. Often, risks will be either positively or negatively correlated to one another. Actions or events will affect correlated risks similarly. For example, reducing the level of problem assets should reduce not only credit risk but also liquidity and reputation risk. When two risks are negatively correlated, reducing one type of risk may increase the other. For example, a bank may reduce overall credit risk by expanding its holdings of one- to four-family residential mortgages instead of commercial loans, only to see its interest rate risk soar because of the interest rate sensitivity and optionality of the mortgages.

Lending can expose a bank's earnings and capital to all of the risks. Therefore, it is important that the examiner assigned LPM understands all the risks embedded in the loan portfolio and their potential impact on the institution. How each of these categories relates to a bank's lending function is detailed in the following sections.

Credit Risk

For most banks, loans are the largest and most obvious source of credit risk. However, there are other pockets of credit risk both on and off the balance sheet, such as the investment portfolio, overdrafts, and letters of credit. Many products, activities, and services, such as derivatives, foreign exchange, and cash management services, also expose a bank to credit risk.

The risk of repayment, i.e., the possibility that an obligor will fail to perform as agreed, is either lessened or increased by a bank's credit risk management practices. A bank's first defense against excessive credit risk is the initial credit-granting process – sound underwriting standards, an efficient, balanced approval process, and a competent lending staff. Because a bank cannot easily overcome borrowers with questionable capacity or character, these factors exert a strong influence on credit quality. Borrowers whose financial performance is poor or marginal, or whose repayment ability is dependent upon unproven projections can quickly become impaired by personal or external economic stress. Management of credit risk, however, must continue after a loan has been made, for sound initial credit decisions can be undermined by improper loan structuring or inadequate monitoring.

Traditionally, banks have focused on oversight of individual loans in managing their overall credit risk. While this focus is important, banks should also view credit risk management in terms of portfolio segments and the entire portfolio. The focus on managing individual credit risk did not avert the credit crises of the 1980s. However, had the portfolio approach to risk management augmented these traditional risk management practices, banks might have at least reduced their losses.

Effective management of the loan portfolio's credit risk requires that the board and management understand and control the bank's risk profile and its credit culture. To accomplish this, they must have a thorough knowledge of the portfolio's composition and its inherent risks. They must understand the portfolio's product mix, industry and geographic concentrations, average risk ratings, and other aggregate characteristics. They must be sure that the policies, processes, and practices implemented to control the risks of individual loans and portfolio segments are sound and that lending personnel adhere to them.

Banks engaged in international lending face country risks that domestic lenders do not. Country risk encompasses all of the uncertainties arising from a nation's economic, social, and political conditions that may affect the payment of foreigners' debt and equity investments. Country risk includes the possibility of political and social upheaval, nationalization and expropriation of assets, governmental repudiation of external indebtedness, exchange controls, and currency devaluation or depreciation. Unless a nation repudiates its external debt, these developments might not make a loan uncollectible. However, even a delay in collection could weaken the lending bank.

Transfer risk, which is a narrower form of country risk, is the possibility that an obligor will not be able to pay because the currency of payment is unavailable. This unavailability may be a matter of government policy. For example, although an individual borrower may be very successful and have sufficient local currency cash flow to pay its foreign (e.g., U.S. dollar) debt, the borrower's country may not have sufficient U.S. dollars available to permit repayment of the foreign indebtedness. The transfer risk associated with banks' exposures in foreign countries is evaluated by the Interagency Country Exposure Review Committee (ICERC). For examination purposes, the transfer risk rating assigned to a country by the ICERC applies to all bank assets in that country. However, examiners may classify individual loans and other assets more severely for credit risk reasons.

Strategies for managing country risk will be discussed in "Country Risk Management," a separate booklet in the Comptroller's Handbook.

Interest Rate Risk

The level of interest rate risk attributed to the bank's lending activities depends on the composition of its loan portfolio and the degree to which the terms of its loans (e.g., maturity, rate structure, embedded options) expose the bank's revenue stream to changes in rates.

Pricing and portfolio maturity decisions should be made with an eye to funding costs and maturities. When significant individual credits or portfolio segments are especially sensitive to interest rate risk, they should be periodically stress-tested. If the asset/liability management committee (ALCO), which typically is responsible for managing the bank's interest rate risk, is to manage all of the bank's positions, it must have sufficient reports on loan portfolio and pipeline composition and trends. These reports might include a maturing loans report, pipeline report, and rate and repricing report.

Banks frequently shift interest rate risk to their borrowers by structuring loans with variable interest rates. Borrowers with marginal repayment capacity may experience financial difficulty if the interest rates on these loans increase. As part of the risk management process, banks should identify borrowers whose loans have heightened sensitivity to interest rate changes and develop strategies to mitigate the risk. One method is to require vulnerable borrowers to purchase interest rate protection or otherwise hedge the risk.

The Comptroller's Handbook booklet "Interest Rate Risk" provides guidance on interest rate risk management.

Liquidity Risk

Because of the size of the loan portfolio, effective management of liquidity risk requires that there be close ties to, and good information flow from, the lending function. Obviously, loans are a primary use of funds. And while controlling loan growth has always been a large part of liquidity management, historically the loan portfolio has not been viewed as a significant source of funds for liquidity management. Practices are changing, however. Banks can use the loan portfolio as a source of funds by reducing the total dollar volume of loans through sales, securitization, and portfolio run-off.

In fact, banks are taking a more active role in managing their loan portfolios. While these activities are often initiated to manage credit risk, they have also improved liquidity. Banks increasingly are originating loans "for sale" or securitization. Consumer loans (mortgages, instalment loans, and credit cards) are routinely originated for immediate securitization. Many larger banks have been expanding their underwriting for the syndicated loan market. Additionally, banks are also expanding the packaging and sale of distressed credits and otherwise undesirable loans.

As part of liquidity planning, a bank's overall liquidity strategy should include the identification of those loans or loan portfolio segments that may be easily converted to cash. A loan's liquidity hinges on such characteristics as its quality, pricing, scheduled maturities, and conformity to market standards for underwriting. Loans are also a source of liquidity when used as collateral for borrowings. The ease with which a bank can participate or sell loans to other lenders or investors (and the terms on which the bank can do so) will vary with market conditions, the type of loan, and the quality of loan. Information provided for liquidity analysis should include an assessment of these variables under various scenarios.

Liquidity is also affected by the amount of the bank's commitments to lend and the actual amount that borrowers draw against those commitments. A bank should have systems to track commitments and borrower usage. Knowledge of the types of commitments, deals in the pipeline, normal usage levels, and historically high usage levels are important in assessing whether available liquidity will be adequate for normal, seasonal, or emergency needs. Management information systems should distinguish between commitments that the bank is legally obligated to fund and those (guidance or advisory lines) that it is not.

Any analysis of a bank's ability to reduce or cut existing commitments must consider more than its legal obligation to lend. It should also consider reputation risk and the potential for lender-liability actions. The withdrawal or reduction of commitments can have significant ramifications for a bank. From a strategic perspective, any tightening of commitments may adversely affect a bank's ability to maintain or grow a customer base if it is perceived as an unreliable lender in tight credit markets. A bank's reputation may also suffer if it is perceived as unwilling to support community credit needs. Given these ancillary risks, bank management must carefully assess the implications of curtailing lending lines.

Price Risk

Most of the developments that improve the loan portfolio's liquidity have implications for price risk. Traditionally, the lending activities of most banks were not affected by price risk. Because loans were customarily held to maturity, accounting doctrine required book value accounting treatment. However, as banks develop more active portfolio management practices and the market for loans expands and deepens, loan portfolios will become increasingly sensitive to price risk.

Loans originated for sale as part of a securitization or for direct placement in the secondary market carry price risk while they are in the pipeline awaiting packaging and sale. During that period, the assets should be placed in a "held-for-sale" account, where they must be repriced at the lower of cost or market. The same accounting treatment can apply to syndicated credits and distressed loans. When a bank underwrites a larger portion of a syndicated loan than its "hold" position, the excess portion must be placed in a held-for-sale account. Once a sale strategy is adopted for distressed or otherwise undesirable credits, those credits should also be placed in a held-for-sale account.

Banks engaged in international lending may be affected by price changes in the secondary market for such loans. Each month, banks that actively trade foreign debt must mark to market the loans in their trading account. In addition, banks that have elected to hold so-called "Brady Bonds" as loans must mark them to market in accordance with the requirements of FAS 115.

Foreign Exchange Risk

Foreign exchange risk is present when a loan or portfolio of loans is denominated in a foreign currency or is funded by borrowings in another currency. In some cases, banks will enter into multi-currency credit commitments that permit borrowers to select the currency they prefer to use in each rollover period. Foreign exchange risk can be intensified by political, social, or economic developments. The consequences can be unfavorable if one of the currencies involved becomes subject to stringent exchange controls or is subject to wide exchange-rate fluctuations. Foreign exchange risk is discussed in more detail in "Foreign Exchange," a section of the Comptroller's Handbook.

Transaction Risk

In the lending area, transaction risk is present primarily in the loan disbursement and credit administration processes. The level of transaction risk depends on the adequacy of information systems and controls, the quality of operating procedures, and the capability and integrity of employees. Significant losses in loan and lease portfolios have resulted from inadequate information systems, procedures, and controls. For example, banks have incurred increased credit risk when information systems failed to provide adequate information to identify concentrations, expired facilities, or stale financial statements. At times, banks have incurred losses because they failed to perfect or renew collateral liens; to obtain proper signatures on loan documents; or to disburse loan proceeds as required by the loan documents.

Compliance Risk

Lending activities encompass a broad range of compliance responsibilities and risks. By law, a bank must observe limits on its loans to a single borrower, to insiders, and to affiliates; limits on interest rates; and the array of consumer protection and Community Reinvestment Act regulations. A bank's lending activities may expose it to liability for the cleanup of environmental hazards. A bank may also become the subject of borrower-initiated "lender liability" lawsuits for damages attributed to its lending or collection practices. Supervisory activities should include the review of the bank's internal compliance process to ensure that examiners identify and investigate compliance issues.

Strategic Risk

A primary objective of loan portfolio management is to control the strategic risk associated with a bank's lending activities. Inappropriate strategic or tactical decisions about underwriting standards, loan portfolio growth, new loan products, or geographic and demographic markets can compromise a bank's future. Examiners should be particularly attentive to new business and product ventures. These ventures require significant planning and careful oversight to ensure the risks are appropriately identified and managed. For example, many banks are extending their consumer loan activities to "sub-prime" borrowers. The product may be familiar, but the borrowers' behavior may differ considerably from the banks' typical customer. Do they understand the unique risks associated with this market, can they price for the increased risk, and do they have the technology and MIS to service this market? Moreover, how will they compete with the nonbank companies who dominate this market? Both bankers and examiners need to decide whether the opportunities outweigh the strategic risks. If a bank is considering growing a loan product or business in a market saturated with that product or business, it should make sure that it is not overlooking other lending opportunities with more promise. During their evaluation of the loan portfolio management process, examiners should ensure that bankers are realistically assessing strategic risk.

Reputation Risk

When a bank experiences credit problems, its reputation with investors, the community, and even individual customers usually suffers. Inefficient loan delivery systems, failure to adequately meet the credit needs of the community, and lender-liability lawsuits are also examples of how a bank's reputation can be tarnished because of problems within its lending division.

Reputation risk can damage a bank's business in many ways. The value of the bank's stock falls, customers and community support is lost, and business opportunities evaporate. To protect their reputations, banks often feel that they must do more than is legally required. For example, some banks have repurchased loan participations when credit problems develop, even though these problems were not apparent at the time of the underwriting.

Credit Culture and Risk Profile

Understanding the credit culture and the risk profile of the bank is central to successful loan portfolio management. Because of the significance of a bank's lending activities, the influence of the credit culture frequently extends to other bank activities. Staff members throughout the bank should understand the bank's credit culture and risk profile. The knowledge should pass from the chief credit policy officer to account officers to administrative support. Directors and senior management should not only publicly endorse the credit standards that are a credit culture's backbone but should also employ them when formulating strategic plans and overseeing portfolio management.

A bank's credit culture is the sum of its credit values, beliefs, and behaviors. It is what is done and how it is accomplished. The credit culture exerts a strong influence on a bank's lending and credit risk management. Values and behaviors that are rewarded become the standards and will take precedence over written policies and procedures.

A bank's risk profile is more measurable than its credit culture. A risk profile describes the various levels and types of risk in the portfolio. The profile evolves from the credit culture, strategic planning, and the day-to-day activities of making and collecting loans. Developing a risk profile is no simple matter. For example, two banks with identical levels of classified loans can have quite different profiles. Bank A's classified loans might be fully secured and made to borrowers within its local market, while bank B's loans are out-of-market, unsecured loan participations. Consider, as well, how much more the failure of a $3 million loan would hurt a $500 million bank than a $5 billion bank. The risk profile will change over time as portfolio composition and internal and external conditions change.

Credit culture varies from bank to bank. Some banks approach credit very conservatively, lending only to financially strong, well-established borrowers. Growth-oriented banks may approach lending more aggressively, lending to borrowers who pose a higher repayment risk. These cultural differences are grounded in a bank's objectives for asset quality, growth, and earnings. Emphasizing one of these objectives over another does not, in and of itself, preclude achieving satisfactory performance in all three. However, the emphasis will influence how lending activities are conducted and may prompt changes in credit policies and risk control systems. For example, a bank driven to achieve aggressive growth targets may require more detailed credit policies and more controlling administrative and monitoring systems to manage credit risk properly. Consistently successful banks achieve a balance between asset quality, growth, and earnings. They have cultural values, credit policies, and processes that reinforce each other and that are clearly communicated, well understood, and carefully followed.

The culture, risk profile, and credit practices of a bank should be linked. If the credit practices and risk-taking activities of a bank are inconsistent with the desired culture and policies, management should find out why and initiate change to bring them back in balance. When practices do not correspond to policies, lenders may not clearly understand the culture, credit controls may not be effective, policies and systems may be inappropriate for the credit environment, or employees may be rewarded for behaviors that are different from those advanced by policy. If the risk profile deviates from cultural norms, management should reassess the limits, policies, and practices.

Senior management and the board should periodically evaluate the bank's credit culture and risk profile. Are marketing plans and financial budgets consistent with credit risk objectives? Do lender compensation programs reward performance that promotes strong credit quality? Do employees' behaviors demonstrate their understanding of the culture? Because the credit culture influences every aspect of the credit process, management should regularly confirm that the culture is consistent with the desired appetite for risk. Independent audit and internal loan review functions should help with this assessment.

Significant cultural confusion can surface in merged and acquired companies. Integrating credit cultures can prove time-consuming and difficult. Efforts to force or hasten the transition are often disruptive. Banks should test frequently to discover whether staff members are being assimilated into the credit culture and whether the culture is consistent with policy. This can be accomplished informally by talking to staff members, or more formally by reviewing recommendations, such as new loan proposals or exceptions, to ensure that the staff's actions reflect the desired culture.

Loan Portfolio Objectives

Loan portfolio objectives establish specific, measurable goals for the portfolio. They are an outgrowth of the credit culture and risk profile. The board of directors must ensure that loans are made with the following three basic objectives in mind:

- To grant loans on a sound and collectible basis.
- To invest the bank's funds profitably for the benefit of shareholders and the protection of depositors.
- To serve the legitimate credit needs of their communities.

Strategic Planning for the Loan Portfolio

For most banks, meeting these three objectives will require that senior management and the board of directors develop medium- and long-term strategic plans and objectives for the loan portfolio. These strategies should be consistent with the strategic direction and risk tolerance of the institution. They should be developed with a clear understanding of their risk/reward consequences. They also should be reviewed periodically and modified as appropriate. In drawing up strategic objectives, management and the board should consider establishing:

- What proportion of the balance sheet the loan portfolio should comprise.
- Goals for loan quality.
- Goals for portfolio diversification.
- How much the portfolio should contribute to the bank's financial objectives.
- Loan product mix.
- Loan growth targets by product, market, and portfolio segment.
- Product specialization.
- What the bank's geographic markets should be.
- Targeted industries.
- Targeted market share.
- Community needs and service.
- General financial objectives (e.g., increase fee income).

The bank's loan policies, underwriting guidelines, and procedures should communicate and support the strategic objectives for the portfolio. MIS should be able to inform management about whether performance measures up to plans. Management should evaluate business, marketing, and compensation plans to ensure that short-term goals and incentives are consistent with strategic portfolio objectives and risk tolerances.

In community banks without formal strategic plans, senior management should be able to articulate the bank's strategic objectives. It should be evident, as well, that the board of directors has endorsed those objectives.

Financial Goals

Business plans or budgets detailing the financial goals for the loan portfolio are the next step in the strategic planning and goal setting process. Business plans should set realistic financial goals that are consistent with strategic goals and risk tolerance levels. Bankers and examiners should be alert to aggressive financial goals because they generally require high growth and increased risk-taking.

Banks typically assess their financial performance using measurements such as earnings, return on equity, and return on assets. Financial performance measures should also consider the relationship between risk and return.

Banks should assess the risk/return relationship at both the individual loan and portfolio level. While more sophisticated loan pricing models include multiple factors to differentiate risk, smaller banks can get acceptable results with basic models relating a few variables — loan income to capital, for example. Banks increasingly are measuring the financial performance of loan portfolios by their risk-adjusted returns. The OCC encourages banks to incorporate more risk/reward analysis into their loan underwriting decisions and portfolio management practices.

Risk Tolerance

In addition to establishing strategic objectives for the loan portfolio, senior management and the board are responsible for setting risk limits on the bank's lending activities. Risk limits should take into consideration the bank's historical loss experience, its ability to absorb future losses, and the bank's desired level of return. Limits may be set in various ways, individually and in combination. For example, they may be applied to a characteristic of individual loans, to the volume of a particular segment of the loan portfolio, and to the composition of the portfolio as a whole. Limits on loans to certain industries or on certain segments of the portfolio should be set with an eye to their impact on the portfolio's aggregate risk. In other words, as some limits are raised, it may be necessary to lower others to maintain the desired overall level of risk. Limits should be based on the interrelationship of risk and reward and on the risk to capital, earnings, or both.

The bank should have a system in place to ensure that exposures approaching risk limits are brought to the attention of senior management and the board. Both on- and off-balance-sheet exposure should be included in the risk limit measurement system. Exceeding or modifying established risk limits should require their explicit approval. In addition, any proposed changes to the bank's underwriting standards should be evaluated to determine how the change will affect overall portfolio risk.

Portfolio Risk and Reward

Banking is both a risk-taking and profit-making business, and bank loan portfolios should return profits commensurate with their risk. Although this concept is intellectually sound and almost universally accepted by bankers and examiners alike, banks have had difficulty implementing it. Over the years, volatility in banks' earnings usually has been linked to the loan portfolio. While there are many contributing factors including market forces, anxiety for income, poor risk measurement, and weak risk management, a common underlying factor has been banks' tendency to underestimate or underprice credit risk. Because bank managements and boards are responsible for serving their communities, achieving acceptable shareholder returns, and protecting the interests of depositors, they need to ensure that the loan portfolio provides consistent, reasonable returns. Individual credits and portfolio segments should be priced to provide reasonable shareholder returns while maintaining adequate capital and allowance levels.

The price (index rate, spread, and fees) charged for an individual credit should cover funding costs, overhead/administrative expenses, the required profit margin (generally expressed as a return on assets or equity), and risk. Funding costs are relatively easy to measure and incorporate into loan pricing. Measuring overhead and administrative costs is more complicated because banks traditionally have not had strong cost accounting systems. Additionally, common services with differing or ambiguous values to each user (What, for example, is the dollar value of loan review?) can be difficult to measure. The required profit margin is a straightforward concept and is usually derived from the strategic plan.

This leaves "risk," which is the crux of the pricing dilemma. The methods used to incorporate risk into loan pricing decisions range from simple "pro-rata" allocations of existing loan loss reserves and capital to complex estimations of default frequency and probability, loss levels, and loss volatility. Recent developments in credit and portfolio risk measurement and modeling are improving banks' ability to measure and price risk more precisely and are facilitating the management of capital and the allowance for loan and lease losses. However, these methods require accurate risk measurement at the individual loan level and robust portfolio risk MIS.

Even with these developments, the loan pricing decision is clouded. Banks often incorporate other revenues attributed to the lending "relationship" into the loan pricing decision. The lending relationship has been, and continues to be, used to win other business with the customer (cash management services, F/X and derivatives sales, custody, etc.). Relationship pricing and profitability measures are important tools for managing credit and portfolio returns. These concepts are increasingly used to identify profitable business opportunities and to cull lending relationships whose returns are insufficient relative to risk. Both bankers and examiners, however, must be alert to inappropriate application of relationship pricing and return methods. Loans may be booked at unprofitable rates based on the assumption, or promise, that other profitable business will follow. When the other business fails to materialize, the returns may be insufficient to compensate the bank for the credit risk. Banks should have systems to accurately measure relationship returns, and must exercise tight controls over loans granted on the basis that relationship profitability will be achieved in the future.

Portfolio risk and return concepts encompass almost all of the credit risk measurement and management principles discussed throughout this booklet. Ultimately, the risks in individual credits, lending relationships, portfolio segments, and entire portfolios will be incorporated into pricing decisions through discrete risk-based allowance and capital charges. For now, pricing for risk continues to be a developing science. Banks are encouraged to develop sufficient systems to measure and price risk within credits and portfolios accordingly.

The Loan Policy

The loan policy is the primary means by which senior management and the board guide lending activities. Although the policy primarily imposes standards, it also is a statement of the bank's basic credit philosophy. It provides a framework for achieving asset quality and earnings objectives, sets risk tolerance levels, and guides the bank's lending activities in a manner consistent with the bank's strategic direction. Loan policy sets standards for portfolio composition, individual credit decisions, fair lending, and compliance management.

Loan policies vary in length, organization, degree of detail, and breadth of topics – there is no ideal format. Frequently, the bank's general lending policy will be supplemented by more detailed underwriting standards, guidelines, and procedures. [N.B. Hereafter, references to loan policy should be interpreted to include these supplements.] Within the same banking company, certain aspects of the policy may vary because of factors such as geographic location, economic conditions, personnel, or portfolio objectives. The format should be tailored to fit the needs of a particular bank, and the scope and detail should be commensurate with the complexity of the bank's lending activities.

In all but very small community banks, the loan policy will be written. The policy should provide a realistic description of where the bank wants to position itself on the risk/reward spectrum. It needs to provide sufficient latitude for a bank to respond to good business opportunities while concurrently controlling credit risk. In normal circumstances, a bank should be able to achieve portfolio objectives and respond to changing market conditions without triggering a limit. Limits should not be so conservative that insignificant changes breach them, nor should they be so liberal that they have no practical effect.

For the policy to be an effective risk management tool, it must clearly establish the responsibilities of those involved in the lending process. For example, who is authorized to approve a covenant violation, who arbitrates risk rating differences, can a credit-scored decision be overridden? Lenders must know what is expected of them. When policy is vague or too broad, credit standards may be unclear and virtually nothing may be regarded as an exception. If the policy states that a bank will extend credit to established businesses, almost any company would qualify. But a policy further requiring the business to be profitable, in operation for at least two years, and located within the bank's community is providing meaningful guidance. When policy is too prescriptive and particular, exceptions to policy will become the rule and meaningless exception data will mask meaningful trends, thereby diminishing the effectiveness of the policy.

Because exceptions are so important, the policy should address them specifically; it should state when they are acceptable and how they should be identified, mitigated, and documented. Some lending standards, such as those that implement legal requirements or those whose violation quickly translates into losses, have greater significance than others. More substantive exceptions should have heightened reporting requirements to senior management and the board. Failure to comply with the provisions of loan policy concerning exceptions is generally regarded as a material weakness.

Significant numbers of material exceptions should be a factor in a lender's performance evaluation.

Policies should be periodically reviewed and revised to accommodate changes in the bank's strategic direction, risk tolerance, or market conditions. Policy review should consider the organizational structure, breadth and complexity of lending activities, capabilities and skills of lending personnel, and strategic portfolio quality and earnings objectives. Changes in regulations and business conditions also need to be considered. In addition to providing an opportunity for change, the review should evaluate how well the policy has guided lending decisions. For example, a high volume of exceptions indicates that many loan decisions are being made outside the policy. This could mean that the bank is assuming more risk than is desirable or that the policy is too restrictive. If the bank's policy is too restrictive, easing it could increase business opportunities without unduly increasing risk. Conversely, the absence of exceptions may indicate that the policy is too vague, and a tightening of the policy could strengthen the controls on loan quality. All policy reviews should include the organizational unit responsible for assessing compliance with policy.

Loan Policy Topics

While the form and contents of loan policies and procedures will vary from bank to bank, there are some topics that should be covered in all cases. These are:

- Loan authorities.
- Limits on aggregate loans and commitments.
- Portfolio distribution by loan category and product.
- Geographic limits.
- Desirable types of loans.
- Underwriting criteria.
- Financial information and analysis requirements.
- Collateral and structure requirements.
- Margin requirements.
- Pricing guidelines.
- Documentation standards.
- Collections and charge-offs.

- Reporting requirements.
- Guidelines for loan participations.
- Off-balance-sheet exposure.

These topics are described in more detail in appendix A.

The policy may also address insider transactions, affiliate transactions, conflicts of interest, the code of ethics, community support, appraisal requirements, environmental assessment requirements, relevant accounting issues (such as charge-off loans, nonperforming loans, and debt restructuring), and the allowance for loan and lease losses. Any administrative requirements for granting loans should be covered in the policy. Policies and procedures should also ensure compliance with laws and regulations.

Loan Approval Process

The loan approval process is the first step towards good portfolio quality. When individual credits are underwritten with sound credit principles, the credit quality of the portfolio is much more likely to be sound. Although good loans sometimes go bad, a loan that starts out bad is likely to stay that way. The foremost means to control loan quality is a solid loan approval process.

The OCC does not recommend any particular system of loan approval. However, every loan approval process should introduce sufficient controls to ensure acceptable credit quality at origination. The process should be compatible with the bank's credit culture, its risk profile, and the capabilities of its lenders. Further, the system for loan approvals needs to establish accountability.

Each method of loan approval has inherent strengths and weaknesses. The committee method is advantageous because knowledge can be shared, but it may diminish accountability and often slows a bank's responsiveness. The individual signature authority system is more timely and establishes clear accountability, but it can create undue credit risk if a lender's knowledge and experience are inadequate to his or her authority. Laddered or joint authorities, variations that some banks employ, combine elements of both systems. The involvement of an independent loan approval authority whose primary goal is quality (such authority might be invested in a senior credit officer or credit administrator) is also a method to introduce more objectivity to the loan approval process. Whatever approach or combination of approaches a bank uses, internal control mechanisms are necessary to ensure that the approval system produces sound credit decisions.

An effective loan approval process establishes minimum requirements for the information and analysis upon which a credit decision is based. It provides guidance on the documents needed to approve new credit, renew credit, increase credit to existing borrowers, and change terms in previously approved credits. It will also designate who has the authority to approve credit or changes in credit terms. Loan authorities should be commensurate with the experience of the lender/credit officer and take into consideration the type of credit, the amount of credit, and the level of risk involved.

Generally, underwriting document standards should include:

- Financial information including:
    - current and historical balance sheet and income data,
    - balance sheet, income, and cash flow projections, when appropriate, and
    - comparative industry data when appropriate.
- Financial analysis, including repayment capacity.
- Collateral identification and valuation.
- Guarantor support and related financial information.
- Summary of borrower and affiliated credit relationships.
- Loan terms, including tenor and repayment structure.
- Pricing information, including relationship profitability data.
- Covenants and requirements for future submission of financial data.
- Exceptions to policy and underwriting guidelines and mitigants.
- Information fields to capture data for concentration reporting, identifying SNCs (shared national credits), etc.
- Risk rating or recommended risk rating.

The approval process for consumer loans may be more streamlined, but should still include sufficient information to support the credit granting decision, including, when applicable, scorecard data.

Portfolio Management

Oversight

To properly administer the loan portfolio, the bank should clearly define the roles and responsibilities of management. Typically, one person or group is responsible and authorized to take the steps necessary to assure that risk in the portfolio stays within acceptable bounds. Since this goal can be accomplished by a variety of structures, the OCC does not favor any particular one – the best system is the one that meets the bank's needs.

Risk Identification

Effective risk identification starts with the evaluation of individual credits. Rating the risk of each loan in timely credit evaluations is fundamental to loan portfolio management. Some banks apply risk ratings to relationships, others prefer to rate each facility, and still others rate both relationships and facilities. All of these approaches are acceptable to the OCC. Risk ratings should also be applied to off-balance-sheet exposures like letters of credit and unfunded commitments that the bank is obligated to fund unless there is a default. These evaluations allow the prompt detection of changes in portfolio quality, enabling management to modify portfolio strategies and intensify the supervision of weaker credits in a timely manner.

In grading loans for supervisory purposes, the OCC uses five categories: pass, special mention, substandard, doubtful, and loss. Banks are encouraged to use these regulatory classifications as a foundation for their own risk rating systems. The OCC further encourages banks to expand their risk ratings for "pass" credits. Using multiple ratings to differentiate the risks of "pass" credits facilitates portfolio risk measurement and analysis, pricing for risk, and early warning objectives. The number of additional ratings used will vary from bank to bank and will depend on the bank's own risk management objectives.

After each loan has been risk rated, the ratings of individual credits should be reviewed, and they should be analyzed in the context of the portfolio segment and the entire portfolio. The analysis should ensure that ratings are consistently applied and should consider trends, migration data, and weighted average risk ratings. Risk ratings, when used in conjunction with other information (such as exception levels, past-due trends, and loan growth), can produce an instructive picture of asset quality and credit risk. Risk ratings can help the bank's portfolio managers in other ways as well — when they set underwriting standards, asset diversification goals, and pricing levels, for example.

Loan policy should designate who is accountable for the accuracy of risk ratings. The account officer is a logical choice because he or she knows more about the credit than anyone else and should have access to timely financial information from the borrower. Assigning the account officer risk rating responsibility heightens his or her accountability for credit quality and has derivative benefits for loan approvals and account management. Some banks assign risk rating responsibility to a credit officer, loan review officer, or a more senior bank officer. While these officers may be more objective and experienced, they may be less sensitive to subtle changes in the borrower's condition, and their ratings changes may be less timely. Perhaps most important, making someone other than the account officer accountable may diminish his or her sense of responsibility for identifying and controlling credit risk.

A process should be in place to ensure that risk ratings are updated in a timely fashion and that appropriate changes are made anytime there is a significant occurrence. Absent such an event, the frequency of risk rating analysis should be a function of the loan's complexity and quality, the portfolio's risk characteristics, and the quality of the lending staff. At a minimum, risk rating evaluations should be conducted annually. More frequent attention should be given to certain kinds of credits — criticized loans, loans to borrowers in a troubled industry, and loans supervised by an inexperienced or weak lender, for example. All risk ratings should be reassessed when significant new information is received. Risk rating analyses should be coordinated with analyses of the allowance for loan and lease losses.

Management should systematically verify account officers' risk ratings. In larger banks, an independent loan review department usually evaluates the ratings; in smaller banks, senior managers who are not involved in credit decisions or a loan review officer (full-time or part-time) can evaluate samples. Small banks can also outsource the evaluation. Whatever system is selected, it should reflect the complexity and size of the portfolio and be independent of the lending function. Each account officer's performance evaluation should take into account the accuracy of his or her risk ratings.

Because of their importance, risk identification system concepts and risk rating accuracy are discussed in several sections of this booklet and in other handbook booklets. For additional information please refer in the Comptroller's Handbook to "Classification of Credits: Domestic and International" and "Allowance for Loan and Lease Losses," as well as the booklets that address specialized lending.

Exceptions to Policy, Procedures, and Underwriting Guidelines

Lending exceptions generally either relate to documentation or underwriting. Banks should have systems to analyze and control both types of exceptions. While it is advisable to identify, mitigate, and monitor all exceptions, the level of attention and reporting should correspond with the materiality of the exception. A missing title can be handled satisfactorily at the administrative level, but a breach of the house lending limit should be brought to the attention of senior management and the board. Institutions making "low documentation" small business and farm loans are exempt from exception tracking for the qualifying loans. (For additional information refer to Banking Bulletin 93-18.)

Documentation Exceptions

"Loan documentation" refers broadly to the documents needed to legally enforce the loan agreement and properly analyze the borrower's financial capacity. When a document is missing, stale, or improperly executed, it becomes an exception. Common loan documents are promissory notes, note guarantees, financial statements, collateral agreements, and appraisals. The promissory note, guarantee, and financial statement must be properly prepared and signed; the financial statement must be received and analyzed in a timely manner by the bank; and the collateral agreement must be recorded in the appropriate jurisdiction.

Documentation exceptions can exacerbate problem loans and seriously hamper work-out efforts. For example, failure to ensure that financial information is received and reviewed in a timely manner can preclude the early identification of potential problems and the opportunity to give those problems immediate attention. Failure to promptly review financial information can delay the identification of covenant violations, which may jeopardize the enforceability of the loan agreement. Neglecting to renew a UCC filing can turn a secured credit into an unsecured credit.

In most banks, loan administration is the control point for loan documentation. A bank should systematically identify document exceptions, initiate timely resolution, and ensure that documentation remains current and valid throughout the loan term. Pre-closing reviews by the lender or attorney and post-closing reviews by loan administration will surface most deficiencies. Needless to say, document exceptions are much easier to rectify before a loan is funded. Banks should analyze document exception patterns to identify problems in the origination process as well as to identify officers, units, or geographic locations that need to strengthen their compliance with policies on documentation. The effectiveness of this control function should be reviewed by audit and loan review.

Policy and Underwriting Exceptions

Policy and underwriting exceptions are conditions in approved loans that violate the loan policy or underwriting guidelines. Because underwriting guidelines are the primary means by which the bank steers lending decisions toward planned strategic objectives and maintains desired levels of risk within the portfolio, deviations from these guidelines should be well documented and justified.

Banks serve a broad constituency. In order to meet the legitimate credit needs of their communities and service creditworthy borrowers, banks will occasionally approve loans outside established guidelines. Loans with approved exceptions are often acceptable risks and should not be criticized solely because of their exceptions. However, these credits often warrant closer-than-normal supervision.

Identifying and approving exceptions is part of effective portfolio risk management. The loan approval document should clearly identify exceptions and provide mitigants that justify the decision to underwrite. This information should be kept in the permanent loan file.

Aggregate Exception Tracking and Reporting

Tracking the aggregate level of exceptions helps detect shifts in the risk characteristics of loan portfolios. In consumer lending, where such tracking is common, it has facilitated risk evaluation, strengthened portfolio liquidity, and helped management to identify new business opportunities. Similar benefits can accrue from tracking underwriting exceptions in commercial and real estate loan portfolios.

When viewed individually, underwriting exceptions may not appear to increase risk significantly; exceptions are often well mitigated shortly after the transaction has taken place. However, when aggregated, even well mitigated exceptions can increase portfolio risk significantly. Aggregate exceptions levels should be analyzed regularly and reported to the bank's board of directors. These analyses and reports allow the board and management to evaluate underwriting practices and assess the level of compliance with the general loan policy. An excessive volume or a pattern of exceptions may signal an unintended or unwarranted relaxation of the bank's underwriting practices. If the volume of exceptions is high, the board of directors may be prompted to reconsider its tolerance for risk; to revise the bank's general loan policy to bring it more into line with the bank's credit culture or current market conditions; to place new limits on the aggregate volume of exceptions; or to change the type of exceptions permitted in the bank's loan portfolio. Early identification and analysis of adverse trends in the level of exceptions, whether for a particular department, type of loan, or loan officer will allow the bank to consider appropriate corrective action.

Exceptions pose varying degrees of risk and their relative significance changes as portfolio composition, risk levels, and external conditions change. Over time, the analysis of aggregate exceptions will enable a bank to correlate particular types of loan policy exceptions with a high probability of default. Portfolio managers should compare the performance of "exception" loans with that of loans made within policy guidelines. In consumer portfolios, tracking aggregate exceptions facilitates override and over-limit decisions and aids in controlling underwriting risk.

Since effective exception tracking systems facilitate better risk management, banks are encouraged to establish these systems and to improve them when they can. Supervisory focus should be directed toward the risks that exceptions create in aggregate or individually, rather than on the exceptions themselves. Examiners should determine whether the bank analyzes exceptions in a thorough and timely manner and whether corrective action follows when necessary. While high volumes of exceptions may indicate increased risk, a lack of exceptions to the loan policy may indicate that the policy is too general to set clear limits on underwriting risk. When policy is revised in response to high volumes of exceptions, examiners should assess the implications of the revision and the impact on risk.

Portfolio Segmentation and Risk Diversification

Risk diversification is a basic tenet of portfolio management. Concentrations of credit risk occur within a portfolio when otherwise unrelated loans are linked by a common characteristic. If this common characteristic becomes a common source of weakness for the loans in concentration, the loans could pose considerable risk to earnings and capital.

Identifying Concentrations of Risk

Managing the loan portfolio includes managing any concentrations of risk. By segmenting the portfolio into pools of loans with similar characteristics, management can evaluate them in light of the bank's portfolio objectives and risk tolerances and, when necessary, develop strategies for reducing, diversifying, or otherwise mitigating the associated risks.

For many banks, "portfolio segmentation" has customarily meant dividing the loan portfolio into broad categories by loan types such as commercial and industrial loans, real estate loans, and consumer loans. As segmentation techniques became more sophisticated, banks identified industry concentrations. Although these divisions are a good starting point, the full benefits of portfolio segmentation can be realized only if the bank is able to form segments using a broader range of risk characteristics.

The defining characteristics of some useful segments are readily discernible — borrower's industry, geographic area, collateral, tenor, facility structure, and risk rating, for example. Other examples are: loans to consumers working for the same employer (or in the same industry), loans to commercial companies that are dependent on the same suppliers (or that sell to the same customers), loans with a common purpose or source of repayment (including guarantor support), loans to affiliated borrowers, and loans to industry sectors that are likely to react in a similar manner to a change — for instance, the trucking and airline industries because of their sensitivity to the price of oil. Because loans have multiple characteristics, it would not be unusual for a loan to be included in more than one portfolio segment. A construction loan, for example, might be included in a real estate concentration report, a geographic concentration report, and a report of non-amortizing loans.

Segmenting a portfolio and diversifying risk require comprehensive management information systems. The MIS data base should include both on- and off-balance-sheet credit exposure. If a bank lacks adequate data on each loan or does not possess a system to "slice and dice" the data for analysis, management's ability to manage the loan portfolio is compromised. But identifying the concentration is only half the job; understanding the dynamics of the concentration and how it will behave in different economic scenarios is the other half. As information about a particular concentration is refined, its effect on the portfolio risk profile can be better evaluated. For example, a bank with a concentration in the communications industry should be able to monitor developments within that industry, track the performance of the portfolio segment, and relate developments in that segment to the overall portfolio. Banks should not be taking risks in industries or products they do not understand. Examiners must use their judgment to determine whether a bank's MIS is sufficient to support effective concentration measurement and management.

Evaluating and Managing Concentrations of Risk

Ideally, the overall portfolio composition and the level of risk in the various pools will be consistent with the goals and guidelines established by the bank's directors. However, it is not unusual for one or more pools to raise concern, either because of the risks associated with the loans or because of the sheer volume of loans with similar characteristics.

Each pool should be evaluated individually — that is, as a discrete pool of risk — and as part of the whole — that is, by how it fits into the portfolio and supports loan portfolio goals. A large exposure to one type of borrower or industry may well be less risky than a small exposure to another. The goal is to achieve the desired balance of risk and return for the portfolio as a whole. Management should have performance standards, risk tolerance levels, and business goals for each concentration, and it should be able to relate these to the overall loan portfolio management strategy. 12 CFR 30, "Standards for Safety and Soundness" (appendix B) requires banks to accord adequate consideration to concentrations of credit risk in their underwriting practices.

In some cases, a pool of loans may represent a concentration of risk that is difficult to avoid (or remedy). Smaller banks may, for example, accumulate concentrations of risk because of their more limited geographic market and the nature of the local economy. Larger banks may develop concentrations of risk through mergers, or to gain leverage or build industry expertise. In any case, the bank must decide whether a particular pool of loans represents an undesirable concentration of risk that should be reduced.

Borrowers in a portfolio concentration exhibit similar financial characteristics such as capital sources, repayment sources, and balance sheet structure. Management should identify the common characteristics that influence credit risk. Focusing monitoring efforts on these characteristics simultaneously simplifies and strengthens the supervision of risk within the pool. Stress testing using common financial indicators will determine which pools are most vulnerable to credit risk and require increased attention.

Concentration Management Techniques

Over the past decade, banks, especially large ones, have been adopting more active portfolio management practices. They are expanding their MIS capabilities and strengthening their credit risk management practices. There are a variety of techniques banks can use to manage portfolios and control concentration risk.

The most common tool is setting exposure limits, or ceilings, on concentrations. Diversifying away from a limit can be accomplished by reducing certain exposures or increasing the borrower base. The reduction of exposures begins with a reassessment of individual borrowers' needs and requires considerable discipline. Nonetheless, it can be a useful tool to diversify risk over a larger customer base.

A bank can change the distribution of its assets by increasing the geographic diversification of borrowers; altering the bank's product mix (for example, by reducing commercial lending and increasing consumer lending); or changing the risk profile of the bank's target market (for example, by turning from middle-market, non-investment-grade customers to well-capitalized, investment-grade customers). Asset sales can also be used to manage concentrations. Banks sell whole loans, sell a portion of a loan into syndication, sell participations in a loan, and securitize certain types of loans. Each of these approaches entails risk/reward trade-offs that must be evaluated in light of the bank's strategic objectives.

Recently, banks have begun using credit derivatives to reduce the risk posed by concentrations. Although their usage is modest in all but the largest banks, credit derivatives are gaining acceptance. If appropriately managed, derivatives may be useful as both a risk management tool and an investment opportunity, especially in times of weak loan demand. Banks should strive to understand both the benefits and the risks associated with these instruments. As more research is conducted and their behavior is analyzed in various economic scenarios, both the risks and benefits of credit derivatives will become clearer. Supervision of derivative products is more fully explored in the "Risk Management of Financial Derivatives" booklet of the Comptroller's Handbook.

Stress Testing

In stress testing, a bank alters assumptions about one or more financial, structural, or economic variables to determine the potential effect on the performance of a loan, concentration, or portfolio segment. This can be accomplished with "back of the envelope" analysis or by using sophisticated financial models. The method employed is not the issue, rather the issue is asking that critical "what if" question and incorporating the resulting answers into the risk management process. Stress testing is a risk management concept, and all banks will derive benefits, regardless of the sophistication of their methods, from applying this risk management concept to their loans and portfolios.

Banks commonly employ a form of stress testing when they subject various assets and liabilities to hypothetical "rate shock" scenarios to determine their exposure to changes in interest rates. Similarly, consumer portfolios that are securitized (e.g., mortgages, credit cards, home equity loans) are heavily stress tested during the structuring process to better gauge their risk and to determine the level of credit enhancements.

While many banks use complex interest rate risk and consumer credit models that take into account the interrelationships between many variables simultaneously, less sophisticated testing methods can also be useful. These same principles can also be used for evaluating commercial credit risk. Stress testing for credit risk can be conducted on individual loans and concentrations or other portfolio segments. Key underwriting assumptions or a critical factor common to a particular portfolio are good candidates for stress testing.

The MIS requirements for stress testing portfolios for credit risk can be significant (they vary depending on the individual circumstances and objectives of the institution). But because banks can evaluate the credit risk of individual loans using little technical support, they should do so during their routine credit evaluations. As part of the initial or ongoing credit analysis, the bank can alter financial variables and assess the impact. These results can then be rolled up to the portfolio level to assess the impact on portfolio credit quality. For example, office space rental rates can be altered, which affects the building's cash flow and debt service repayment capacity. Stress testing would allow bank management to determine at what rental rate the project could no longer service its debt. The test results could then be used to identify what percentage of the portfolio is vulnerable to a hypothetical 10 percent decrease in rental rates. As the bank's knowledge of stress testing grows, it can alter a number of related variables at the same time. Not only rental rates but also office vacancy rates can be altered (a correlated change because occupancy rates drive rental rates). Or the bank can analyze the response of a portfolio or portfolio segment to a variety of oil and gas prices or regulated utility rates.

However, as these examples make clear, the usefulness of even simplified stress testing depends on the accuracy of the "model" used to quantify the sensitivity of loan performance to the selected variables. The results of any such stress testing must always be interpreted with caution, because important additional variables, or interrelationships among variables, may have been omitted from the analysis.

Even if the bank cannot attach probabilities to the scenarios, stress tests can reveal the kinds of events that might present problems. Banks should test the debt service coverage of credits whose coverage is thin. Credits in significant loan pool concentrations should also be stress tested as indicators of the strength of those pools. Based on the results of stress testing, management can develop contingency plans for the credits or pools that stress testing indicates are vulnerable. These plans might include increasing supervision, limiting further advances, restricting portfolio growth, devising exit strategies, or hedging portfolio segments.

Credit portfolio stress testing is a relatively new analytical tool and the OCC does not currently require banks to conduct stress tests or to develop or purchase computer models to perform such tests. Bankers are encouraged, however, to expand their capabilities. Banks of all sizes will benefit by supplementing stress testing of individual loans with portfolio stress testing. They may also want to consider credit modeling software as it becomes more refined and readily available for stress testing.

Allowance for Loan and Lease Losses

Banks must have a program to establish and regularly review the adequacy of their allowance for loan and lease losses (ALLL). The ALLL exists to cover any losses in the loan (and lease) portfolio of all banks. As such, adequate management of the allowance is an integral part of managing credit risk. A major function of effective loan portfolio management is establishing and maintaining an effective process to ensure the adequacy of the ALLL. Credit management is normally responsible for developing and implementing a method of determining whether the ALLL is adequate. The method should include periodic assessments of the level of risk in the loan portfolio and an analysis to ensure that the allowance is adequate to absorb inherent losses.

Guidance on assessing the ALLL process and adequacy is included in the ALLL booklet of the Comptroller's Handbook.

Credit Management Information Systems

The effectiveness of the bank's LPM process heavily depends on the quality of management information systems (MIS). Indeed, many of the advancements of contemporary portfolio management are the direct result of the more robust MIS that is available today. At the same time, many banks are frustrated in their efforts to expand portfolio risk management by the limitations of their MIS. Loan portfolio managers and examiners should be active proponents of the continued improvement of credit-related MIS. While a bank's systems or technology often impedes MIS improvement, lack of understanding or poor communications between credit management and systems personnel can also do so.

Credit-related MIS helps management and the board to fulfill their respective oversight roles. Therefore, when assessing MIS-produced credit reports, the examiner should determine whether the users are receiving the right kind of information at the right time. Reports to senior management and the board must be more than a presentation of numbers; they must be analytical in nature and allow the users to draw independent conclusions. For example, a report presenting the level of classified assets has limited value; however, if the report contains historical information and shows the classified asset position relative to capital, it becomes more useful. Similarly, reports on numbers of exceptions to policy are not very useful, but reports on aggregate exceptions as a percentage of industry or specialized lending portfolios may signal a change in risk assumption. Summary data presented in a concise format generally satisfies management's needs. A report should not give management or the board more information than it can understand in the time it has to devote to the topic.

Line lending managers have different requirements than senior management and the board. In order to properly inform such different user groups, a bank requires good systems architecture. An ideal system would enable a banker to query, track, and aggregate in all loan data fields; prepare a standard array of reports; and prepare ad hoc reports. Bank management and examiners should assess the adequacy and accuracy of the bank's MIS based on the size and scope of lending activities and any planned changes in the portfolio.

The best technology can be next to worthless if the data are not accurate. Only if data are updated periodically and out-of-date loan information purged can MIS reports remain accurate and useful. Preserving the reliability of MIS can be especially difficult in banks that are expanding rapidly. Common data integrity problems include incorrect industry codes, failure to report delinquency, incomplete or outdated information on loan participations, failure to archive note origination dates and amounts at renewal or modification, inaccurate underwriting exception capture, lack of clear reports and reporting lines, incorrect risk ratings or failure to archive risk ratings when a change occurs, and omission of off-balance-sheet exposure. Loan review, credit administration, and audit play a vital role in ensuring that data are accurate. When MIS deficiencies or inaccuracies jeopardize or restrict credit risk management practices, examiners will need to identify the root cause and initiate corrective action.

Collections and Work-out

Banks differ on the methods and organization they use to manage problem loans. The responsibilities for such loans may lie with the originating line unit or a specialized work-out division, depending on the loan size or type. Work-out units are usually staffed with specialized work-out lenders. It is not uncommon for the work-out department to be independent from the line lending unit, but the organization should be dictated by the needs of the bank. Credit policy should articulate how a bank will manage problem credits. A separate policy on problem loans often supplements corporate loan policy.

Routine collection activities generally are handled by the account officers or a specialized collection department. When collection problems persist or credit weaknesses become more pronounced and risk ratings deteriorate, many banks find it beneficial to transfer problem loans to a unit that specializes in work-out activity. The additional resources and closer management supervision of a work-out department normally improve results. Although the managerial responsibility for the credit is transferred to work-out, the financial responsibility, i.e., who is charged with any losses, should be retained by the originating unit.

Specialized work-out units can save a bank considerable money especially during an economic downturn. An effective work-out unit can help craft a strategy to return a troubled borrower to financial health. Because of their proficiency with both rehabilitation and exit strategies, work-out personnel should be closely involved in developing strategy for marginally rated borrowers or any problem loans that are supervised by the line account officer. An experienced work-out unit can provide valuable guidance during initial underwriting and restructures that can help to ensure that the bank's return is maximized in the event of default.

Successful loan work-outs depend on early identification of credit weaknesses and adverse credit trends. The bank's credit culture and risk rating system should encourage lenders and managers to identify problem loans in a timely manner. To facilitate early identification, the bank's risk rating system should have ratings grades for loans that are beginning to exhibit increased risk attributes. These ratings should trigger additional oversight and monitoring. Because lenders are often quite reluctant to transfer a credit even after a problem has been identified, banks should be on guard against their lenders' reluctance to lower loan risk ratings. For lenders to surface loan problems at the earliest possible stage, the positive support of senior management and the board is essential. An added benefit of early identification of individual problem loans is the opportunity it affords credit management to identify and address the systemic risks posed by those loans or groups of similar loans.

Managing problem credits is time-consuming (time that a lender could profitably spend on other duties) and requires special knowledge. Many banks require lenders to transfer problem assets to a work-out unit (with provision for documented exceptions). Such an automatic transfer policy enables a bank to ensure that its dealings with troubled borrowers are uniform. In larger banks where a relationship may contain facilities managed by more than one department, it is generally preferable to transfer the entire credit relationship to ensure consistent treatment of the borrower.

An important part of the work-out and collection process is the performance of "post mortem" reviews to better understand how problem loans and losses develop. At least for all larger loans, analysts should compare each loan's terms and characteristics with underwriting guidelines, and they should determine the borrower's financial condition at the time of loan approval, the timeliness of problem identification, the accuracy of collateral evaluation, the effectiveness of financial covenant structure, and adequacy of documentation.

Lending Control Functions

Besides the loan policy, the primary controls over a bank's lending activities are its credit administration, loan review, and audit functions. Independent credit administration, loan review, and audit functions are necessary to ensure that the bank's risk management process, MIS, and internal and accounting controls are reliable and effective. The bank's control functions can also provide senior management and the board with a periodic assessment of how the bank's employees understand its credit culture and whether their behaviors conform to the bank's standards and values.

Independence

Independence is the ability to provide an objective report of facts and to form impartial opinions. Without independence, the effectiveness of control units may be jeopardized. Independence generally requires a separation of duties and reporting lines. However, it should not be assumed that the independence of a control function is solely a function of reporting lines. Independence also depends heavily on the corporate culture's valuing and promoting objective oversight and constructive criticism. No individual or group should be expected to preserve its independence on its own; instead, senior management, the board, the credit culture, and the organizational framework should all support the independence of control units.

Budget constraints can compromise the independence and ultimately the effectiveness of control functions. Control areas are easy targets for expense reduction efforts because they do not generate revenue. But the costs of control functions are relatively small compared with the much greater costs that historically have resulted from their absence. Before reducing staffing levels, coverage, or review cycles for control units, management should carefully assess the risks to the institution. If management and the board choose to make such reductions, they should be prepared to support them in their overall corporate strategic plan.

Credit Policy Administration

Credit policy administration is responsible for the day-to-day supervision of the loan policy. The unit decides whether the policy provides adequate guidance for lending activities, determines whether employees are following loan policy, reports policy violations, and administers policy and underwriting exceptions. If policy needs to be supplemented or modified, credit policy administration drafts the changes. This unit may also assist the account officers with routine account maintenance such as monitoring covenant compliance and ensuring that financial statements are received, spread, and analyzed in a timely manner.

Credit policy administration is responsible for the body of written documents — loan policy, loan procedures, and policy-related credit memorandums — that govern the credit process. The unit should establish a formal process for developing, implementing and reviewing policy directives.

Loan Review

Loan review is a mainstay of internal control of the loan portfolio. Periodic objective reviews of credit risk levels and risk management processes are essential to effective portfolio management. To ensure the independence of loan review, the unit should report administratively and functionally to the board of directors or a standing committee with audit responsibilities. The board or committee approves the unit's operating budget, prepares the performance evaluation for the division's head, approves the unit's strategic and operating plans, acts on the unit's findings, and ratifies administrative matters. While it is not as critical that loan review's administrative lines have independence, the functional lines should not be compromised. The unit's independence — that is, its ability to remain objective during examinations — should be protected.

The LPM examiner should focus on the role and effectiveness of loan review as part of a comprehensive loan portfolio management process. Weaknesses in loan review hamper the entire portfolio management process and may signal the need for more extensive testing during an examination.

Assessment of the loan review function should also include evaluation of its role in assuring the effectiveness of the loan portfolio management process. The loan review function should go beyond transactional testing to include evaluation of how well individual departments perform.

12 CFR 30, Standards for Safety and Soundness (see appendix B), provides that a bank should establish a system of independent, ongoing credit review and the results of the credit reviews should be communicated to management and the board of directors.

Audit

Audit activities in lending departments usually focus on the accounting controls in the administrative support functions. While loan review has primary responsibility for evaluating credit risk management controls, audit will generally be responsible for validating the lending-related models (e.g., loan pricing models, funds transfer pricing, financial analysis software, credit scoring). The logical structure and assumptions, as well as the data and mathematical algorithms used by the models, must be accurate. Audits should be done at least annually and whenever models are revised or replaced.

Administrative and functional reporting lines for the audit function should be similar to those for the loan review function. A full discussion of the OCC's expectations with respect to the bank's audit function can be found in the booklet "Internal and External Audit."

Administrative and Documentation Controls

The responsibilities of credit administration will vary widely from bank to bank. Credit administration is the operations arm of the lending function. For purposes of this booklet, "credit administration" includes the "backroom" functions of loan disbursement, loan processing and billing, lien perfection, and credit and collateral documentation.

Credit administration is an important control mechanism. In fact, the backroom processing functions are often the first line of defense. Weaknesses in credit administration can pose significant safety and soundness issues for the bank. 12 CFR 30, Standards for Safety and Soundness (see appendix B), establishes guidelines for loan documentation practices. Credit administration is normally reviewed periodically by audit, loan review, or both. Concerns about the adequacy of credit administration may signal the need for more extensive testing.

Communication with Senior Management and the Board

Both senior management and the board of directors should receive clear, concise, timely information about the loan portfolio and its attendant risks. Examiners should determine that management has clearly communicated strategic objectives and risk limits to the board and that the board has approved them. Examiners should also ensure that risk measurement and analysis is adequately reported to both senior management and the board.

Reports to senior management should provide sufficient information for independent evaluation of risk and trends. Reports to the board generally should not contain the same level of detail as those provided to senior management, although in the smallest banks management reports may be sufficient for board use. As the size and complexity of the loan portfolio increases, information provided to the directors should be presented in a summary format. Management should provide the board with readily understandable reports on risk levels and trends. At times, individual directors or boards may request supporting detail. Examiners should determine whether the reports' descriptions of loan portfolio risks are sufficient to enable the board and management to exercise their supervisory responsibilities.

A unit independent of the lending function should evaluate the accuracy, completeness, and timeliness of the information in these reports. This evaluation is normally part of loan review or audit activities. Examiners should assure themselves that reports are accurate. The bank should have evidence that it tests reports periodically for accuracy. If concerns exist about internal testing, examiners should conduct sufficient testing to reach an independent supervisory assessment.

Loan Portfolio Management Supervision

Examiners draw conclusions about the quality of a bank's loan portfolio management from their on-site reviews and from continual supervision of the bank's lending departments. The purpose and scope of those reviews are discussed briefly in the sections that follow. During their reviews, examiners should focus on identifying a product's or process's sources and levels of risk rather than on gathering data. Examiners should identify prospective risks as well as existing ones because prospective risks must be evaluated if long-term safety and soundness is to be ensured.

Asset Quality Reviews

In asset quality reviews, examiners test individual loans for quality. Using a sample of loans, they draw conclusions about the quality of loan supervision, the adequacy of the loan infrastructure, and the level of risk in the portfolio. Traditionally, the analysis of individual loans has been used to determine whether risk ratings are accurate and to build conclusions about loan portfolio management. A more dynamic and efficient approach is to simultaneously use the testing to verify risk ratings and test the lending function itself. For example, a review of newly underwritten credits should be structured to assess the risk in the new transactions as well as to test the effectiveness of loan approval and other policies and processes that govern credit quality. While this approach requires careful planning and design, the results provide more comprehensive information.

Asset quality reviews can be used to draw conclusions about underwriting practices, compliance with policy, loan administration, the accuracy of loan information systems, the adequacy of financial and collateral documentation, and the effectiveness of loan control functions. These reviews also reveal whether the bank's lending department is complying with banking law and regulation. The frequency and scope of asset quality reviews should be based on the level and direction of risk and the quality of risk management. The procedures section of this booklet describes factors that should be considered when designing asset quality and other credit examinations.

The evaluation of asset quality for various types of lending is discussed in more detail in Comptroller's Handbook booklets on each type of lending. Definitions of the regulatory risk rating categories for assets and a discussion of their application can be found in the section on "Classification of Credit: Domestic and International."

Asset quality reviews for community banks incorporate many of the same objectives as those in larger banks; however, the analysis is focused more on the results of operations than the methods used to achieve them. These reviews may need to be expanded when management is not effective or the loan portfolio has a high risk profile or worrisome trends.

Targeted Reviews

Targeted reviews are designed to provide information about new products, growth areas, or other areas of lending-related risk. For example, if a bank had significantly increased the outstanding indirect paper for a particular dealer or had recently started an asset-based lending department, it would be appropriate to perform a targeted review of that activity. Although the scope of these reviews is generally narrow, they may be combined with related comprehensive reviews of other areas.

Process Reviews

Examiners perform process reviews to evaluate aspects of loan portfolio management. These reviews examine methods, organization, work flow, responsibility designations, control systems, and MIS. They focus on the root cause of a problem and foster the early recognition of problems. Typically, the reviews include little, if any, testing of individual loans. This type of supervisory effort is an efficient way to evaluate parts of the loan portfolio management process when staffing and time are limited. Using these reviews, examiners can relate a process's design to how it works. Effective loan portfolio processes generally exhibit good design, cautious implementation, and ongoing maintenance. The results of a process review may indicate that a fuller scope review, to include testing of individual loans, is warranted.

Administrative and Documentation Reviews

Administrative and documentation reviews focus on one or more of a variety of lending-related functions, including policy review, loan approval, collection activity, credit MIS, and the "backroom" functions of loan disbursement, lien perfection, and credit and collateral documentation. These activities have been discussed more fully in previous sections.

Compliance Reviews

Examination procedures that test adherence to laws, rulings, and regulations on consumer lending are outlined in the Consumer Compliance Examination booklets. Testing compliance with applicable laws and regulations, however, is not limited solely to compliance examinations. It may be appropriate, depending on the supervisory objectives, to test compliance with particular laws and regulations during an asset quality examination.

Follow-up Evaluations on Management Commitments

Effective supervision requires timely follow-up on identified weaknesses and management's commitments to corrective action. If weaknesses are serious enough, these commitments will be part of a formal administrative action. Follow-up evaluations should be part of the supervisory strategy for every bank. Examination documentation on follow-up evaluations is discussed in detail in the booklets "Bank Supervision Process" and "Large Bank Supervision."

Ongoing Supervision

Ongoing supervision is an integral component of risk-based supervision and complements examination and targeted review activities conducted throughout the supervisory cycle. A primary objective of ongoing supervision is to detect emerging risks within the loan portfolio and identify changes in the bank's culture. The more complex or risky the loan portfolio, the greater the need for frequent, comprehensive oversight. Ongoing supervision is the foundation for examination planning; it keeps examination activities dynamic and enables examiners to respond to changing risk profiles in a timely manner.

A primary task of ongoing supervision is to determine and periodically review CAMELS (capital, asset quality, management, earnings, liquidity, and sensitivity to market risk) ratings. Risk-based supervision requires examiners to integrate conclusions on risk assessment in the conclusions on CAMELS ratings.

In large banks, ongoing supervision of credit risk involves, among other things, periodic meetings with management and analysis of internal and external MIS to identify current and prospective forces that affect the risk profile of the loan portfolio. In smaller institutions when on-site examinations are not being performed, examiners will use the Uniform Bank Performance Report (UBPR) and quarterly telephonic or on-site meetings with management as the primary means of analyzing loan portfolio trends. For both large and small banks, examiners will update the credit risk assessment and determine whether any changes in those assessments will trigger a change in CAMELS ratings. Although LPM activity will primarily affect the credit assessment factors and the asset quality component of the CAMELS rating, the credit profile may also affect the other CAMELS categories.

General Procedures

Assessing a bank's LPM program involves assessing a variety of credit functions and processes (e.g., underwriting, origination, MIS, administration, loan review) rather than evaluating a single process or function as in other examination programs. Therefore, LPM examination procedures are presented in a cross-functional, as opposed to a "drill down," format. The overall LPM evaluation relies on examiner judgment to assign appropriate weights and "ratings" to the interrelated functions and processes that constitute the bank's LPM system.

Planning is important to the effectiveness of an examination. How much planning an examiner is required to do will depend on his or her knowledge of the bank and the loan portfolio. Before establishing scope, the examiner should make a preliminary assessment of the level and direction of risk and the quality of risk management. To make these assessments, the examiner should review reports and discuss with bank management the condition of the portfolio, as well as changes or planned changes since the most recent examination. Allocating sufficient resources and exercising good judgment during the planning phase will maximize examination efficiencies for the OCC and minimize examination burden for the bank. Banks or portfolios in which the quantity of risk is low and the quality of risk management is high will require examinations with a narrower scope than do those with higher, more volatile levels of risk.

Objective: Develop a preliminary assessment about the quantity of risk and the quality of risk management within the loan portfolio, the direction of risk, and how the risk in the loan portfolio affects the aggregate level of risk of the institution. This assessment will be used to set the scope for the loan portfolio management examination.

Note: Much of the following information will be analyzed more completely during the examination process. All of the listed reports may not be available at all banks.

1. Review the following documents to determine the status of previously identified problems related to the loan portfolio:

    ☐ Previous examination reports.
    ☐ Management's responses to previous examination findings and other bank correspondence.
    ☐ Ongoing supervisory comments.
    ☐ Work papers from previous examinations.
    ☐ Loan review reports.
    ☐ Internal and external audit reports.

2. Review and analyze the Uniform Bank Performance Report (UBPR), BERT, and the bank's current risk assessment to identify broad trends within the loan portfolio.

3. Obtain and analyze reports used by management to supervise the loan portfolio. The reports may include:

    ☐ Strategic and business plans for the loan portfolio.
    ☐ Risk rating reports.
    ☐ Problem loan and watch list reports.
    ☐ Delinquency/nonperforming asset reports.
    ☐ Concentration reports.
    ☐ Portfolio size stratification report.
    ☐ Stress test results.
    ☐ List of new products, services, business initiatives.
    ☐ Exception reports.
    ☐ ALLL analysis.
    ☐ Written policy and procedures manuals.
    ☐ Organization charts.

    The analysis should consider:

    •   Growth and acquisitions.

- New products, services, lines of business.
- Management changes.
- Policy and underwriting changes.
- Changes in risk limits.
- Changes in such external factors as:
  - National, regional, and local economy.
  - Industry outlook.
  - Regulatory framework.
  - Technological change.

4.   Discuss with management:

- How management supervises the loan portfolio.
- Any significant changes in policies, procedures, personnel, and control systems.
- Any internal or external factors that could affect the loan portfolio.
- Management's perception of the bank's credit culture.

5.   Based on the findings and analysis resulting from the previous steps and in consultation with the EIC and other appropriate supervisors, determine the scope of the examination. The scope should focus on areas with emerging risk and on those areas of risk of greatest concern. Determine how much testing is necessary. Sample criteria on size and selection, if needed, are discussed in the statistical sampling appendix to the Comptroller's Handbook for National Bank Examiners.

Select from among the following examination procedures the steps necessary to meet examination objectives. Examiners should tailor the procedures to the bank's specific activities and risks. Note: Examiners will seldom be required to complete every step.

6.   As the examination procedures are performed, test for compliance with all applicable laws, rules, and regulations and with established policies. Confirm the existence of appropriate internal controls. Identify any areas that have inadequate supervision or pose undue risk, and discuss with the EIC the need to perform additional procedures or testing.

Quantity of Risk

Conclusion: The quantity of risk is (low, moderate, high).

Objective: To determine the quantity of risk in the loan portfolio, help determine the direction the risk is moving, and aid in the assessment of the aggregate risk within the institution.

Note: "Loan Policy," "Underwriting Guidelines," and "Strategic Factors" are risk management processes through which examiners reach conclusions about the quality of risk management. However, they also exert a strong influence on the quantity of risk and should be considered when drawing a conclusion about the quantity of risk.

Loan Policy

1. Evaluate whether the loan policy provides adequate guidance to control the quantity of credit risk. Consider the following:

    *   Approval process: approval authority, loan committee structure, loan evaluation analysis requirements, exception definition, and exception reporting requirements.

    *   Underwriting: credit standards, loan structure, maturity limits, collateral, pricing, financial information requirements, documentation standards, appraisal requirements, and environmental assessments.

    *   Loan quality monitoring and evaluation: risk rating definitions, risk rating accountability and responsibility, risk analysis requirements, collection and charge-off responsibility, exception reporting, obligor financial reporting.

    *   Portfolio limits and strategic goals: credit culture, asset distribution, aggregate loan limits, desirable loan types, concentrations and

---

concentration limits, distribution goals, and participation guidelines.

- Compliance: insider transactions, conflicts of interest, accounting requirements, legal lending limit, and all other lending-related regulations.

2. Determine whether the quantity of credit risk has changed or is likely to change because of policy changes. Consider:

   - Permissible loans and loan structures,
   - Acceptable customer definition,
   - Acceptable collateral types and coverage levels,
   - Risk limit guidelines and the potential impact if risk limits are reached,
   - Pricing guidelines. Does the bank's pricing policy incorporate risk/return (risk-based pricing) concepts?

3. Review the bank's charge-off policy. Consider:

   - Consistency with regulatory and accounting definitions.
   - Adherence to policy, particularly on exceptions.
   - Responsibility for charging off assets.
   - Timeliness of charge-offs.
   - Senior management and board review of charge-offs.

4. Have clear lines of authority and responsibility for monitoring adherence to policies, procedures, and limits been established by the board and senior management?

5. Analyze the level and composition of policy exceptions and determine the potential impact on the quantity of risk.
   Note: A bank's lack of an internal tracking system may require examiners to test for adherence to policy.

Underwriting

1. Review the current underwriting guidelines. Assess how changes since the previous examination have affected the quantity of risk. Consider:

   - Customer size standards, external ratings, credit scores, and credit history;
   - Debt service coverage, methods of calculating cash flow, debt/income ratios;
   - Leverage standards, liquidity standards, and other covenant requirements;
   - Amortization requirements, maturity standards;
   - Collateral coverage and collateral valuation;
   - Guarantor standards; and
   - Reporting requirements.

2. Evaluate the bank's analysis when considering a credit application. Consider:

   - Purpose of loan,
   - Loan structure,
   - Borrower's repayment capacity,
   - Collateral requirements,
   - Portfolio goals and limits.

3. Analyze the level, composition, and trend of underwriting exceptions and determine the impact on the quantity of risk.
   Note: A bank's lack of an internal tracking system may require examiners to test for adherence to policy.

Portfolio Composition and Strategic Factors

1. Analyze the composition and changes to the loan portfolio, including off-balance-sheet exposure, since the previous examination. Determine the implications for risk of the following:

- Any significant growth or shift in relative size of key loan segments.
- Material changes in the portfolio or key portfolio segments to include:
    - Elevated risk levels or high growth.
    - Changes and trends in problem, classified, past-due, nonaccrual, and nonperforming assets; charge-off volumes; and risk rating distribution.
- Any significant concentrations, including individual, industry, geographic, and product concentrations.

2. Review unfunded commitments and other "pipeline" reports to determine the potential effect on the loan portfolio's risk profile.

3. Evaluate the credit risk implications of concentrations. Consider the volume and trend of:

- Outstandings.
- Risk rating stratification.
- Exceptions (underwriting, policy, documentation).
- Management expertise
- Economic factors.

4. Determine whether new products have been introduced since the last examination. Analyze their growth and potential effect on credit risk.

5. If the bank has acquired other institutions or loan portfolios, analyze the effect these purchases have had on the portfolio's composition and risk profile. Consider changes to risk rating stratification, concentrations, new obligor types, specialized credits, new loan types, and pricing mechanisms.

6. Review and analyze management-prepared portfolio risk assessments. Consider changes in risk quantification measurements and the underlying causes of these changes.

7. Review the business and/or strategic plan for the loan portfolio. Evaluate how implementation of the plan will affect the quantity of credit risk. Consider:

    - Growth goals and potential sources of new loans;
    - Growth outside the current market area;
    - New products and business lines;
    - Emphasis on high risk products, customers, or industries;
    - Concentrations of credit;
    - Risk limits; and
    - Loss forecasts.

8. Compare portfolio performance with planned performance and ascertain the risk implications.

9. Assess the impact of the bank's asset securitization and loan purchase/sale programs on the quantity of risk. Consider:

    - The magnitude of these programs and their relative significance to overall portfolio composition.
    - The quality of the loans in the program.
    - Probability of, and potential impact if, loans are returned to the bank's balance sheet.
    - The revenues associated with these activities.

10. If the bank employs credit derivatives or other concentration management tools to control credit exposures, analyze their impact on the quantity of risk. Consider:

    - The objectives of these programs.
    - The volume of credit derivatives or similar products.

11. If the bank has developed portfolio diversification targets, evaluate whether they have reduced portfolio risk.

Internal Controls

1. Review recent loan review and loan-related audit reports. If there are any adverse trends in quantitative measures of risk or control weaknesses reported, comment on whether and how much they may increase risk.

2. Analyze the level, composition, and trend of documentation exceptions and determine the potential risk implications.
   Note: A bank's lack of an internal tracking system may require examiners to test for adherence to policy.

3. Evaluate the level of compliance with laws, rules, and regulations applicable to the lending function. Relate the level of compliance to the quantity of credit risk.

External Factors

1. Review the local, regional, and national economic trends and assess their impact on loan portfolio risk levels.

2. Evaluate the results of any stress testing of the loan portfolio or portfolio segments. Include review of testing for changes in interest rates, commodity prices, collateral valuations (such as real estate prices or company valuations based on multiple formulas) or product pricing declines due to competition or statutory rate controls.

3. Assess the bank's exposure to any pending legislative, regulatory, or accounting changes that will materially affect the loan portfolio.

Quality of Risk Management

Conclusion: The quality of risk management is (weak, acceptable, or strong).

Objective: To determine the quality of risk management for the loan portfolio and its impact on the direction of risk and the aggregate level of risk within the institution.

Policy and Strategic Planning

1. Determine whether management has clearly communicated loan portfolio strategic objectives and risk limits to the board of directors and whether the board has approved these goals. In coordination with the assessment of the overall strategic plan, do the following:

    -   Determine whether the reports to senior management and the board of directors provide sufficient information to evaluate risk levels and trends.
    -   Assess the format and clarity of planning reports. Are they easy to understand and interpret?
    -   Assess the board's and senior management's ability to fulfill their oversight roles using the reports.
    -   Evaluate the system used to test the accuracy of planning reports. Management's testing should be thorough and periodic.

2. Determine whether planning activities consider credit culture and loan policy issues and are linked to business plans and budgets. Assess the following:

    -   The consistency between the stated or implied cultural philosophy and the objectives in the strategic plan.
    -   The review process for budgets, business plans, and strategic plans to ensure that they are consistent and achievable.
    -   The process to evaluate the plan's implications for risk.

---

3. Compare actual performance of portfolio(s) with planned performance. Verify that the board of directors and senior management routinely compare performance with planned performance. Evaluate the board's and senior management's review.

4. Evaluate the MIS used to make the foregoing comparison. Do performance reports address the following subjects?

   - Earnings and capital relative to risk measurements and objectives.
   - Pricing objectives.
   - Market share objectives.
   - Diversification goals.
   - Credit quality goals.
   - Community service goals.
   - Nonfinancial objectives.

5. In coordination with the overall evaluation of the strategic plan, evaluate the lending function's planning process for thoroughness and reasonableness. Do plans consider internal strengths and weaknesses, as well as external opportunities and threats?

6. Review the bank's strategic plan for loan portfolio. The following factors should be addressed:

   - Loan portfolio share of the balance sheet.
   - Loan quality goals.
   - Portfolio diversification goals.
   - Loan product mix.
   - Loan growth targets for significant products, customers, and industries.
   - Product specialization.
   - Identification of target markets and industries.
   - Growth and market share goals.
   - External factors.

7. Determine whether the loan planning process provides for periodic reassessments, modifications, or reaffirmations of strategic objectives.

8.   Assess the process for making changes to the portfolio plan. Determine whether changes have been made, and analyze the changes to the plan.

9.   Evaluate the bank's business, marketing, and compensation plans in the lending area to ensure that short-term goals and incentives do not promote behaviors that are inconsistent with strategic portfolio objectives and established risk tolerances. Determine whether management conducted a similar analysis.

10. Assess the loan policy to determine whether it provides appropriate guidance for the bank's lending activities. Consider:

     • Approval process and authority levels.
     • Delivery system/distribution channel.

11. Evaluate how the policy establishes responsibility and accountability for various lending activities. Consider:

     • Approval process.
     • Risk rating process.
     • Exception and over-limit process.
     • Loan closing procedures.
     • Nonaccrual and charge-off process.
     • Allocation process.

12. Evaluate the policy's suitability to any planned changes in lending (e.g., expanding into a new line of business or introducing a new product).

13. Are risk limits well-defined and reasonable? Consider the way these limits are measured (Are capital and earnings at risk used to define the risk limit?) and the impact on the bank if the risk limit is reached.

14. Review the process employed to establish risk limits. Consider management's objectives in setting risk limits.

15. Determine how compliance with risk limits is monitored and reported to senior management and the board of directors.

16. Assess the level of review for credit exposures nearing their risk limits. Is there sufficient reporting to senior managers and is supervision heightened?

17. Evaluate the policy review process to ensure that the policy will change with changes in practices or the external environment, such as increases in risk for a particular product or industry.

18. Determine whether the board of directors has approved the loan policy and whether the policy articulates the desired credit culture.

Processes

Underwriting

1. Determine whether the bank uses underwriting guidelines to better define their credit risk limits. Assess the compatibility of the guidelines with the loan policy and the strategic plan.

2. Determine whether automated loan decision or customer solicitation models are used by lending management.

   - Is the model based on the institution's history or on a national composite?
   - What is the model's design? Were credit-related factors analyzed and used in its development?
   - Does management understand the model and its application? What are the implications of the model's use?
   - Has management made a thorough and accurate assessment of the model's use? Is MIS adequate? Consider asset quality, acceptance rate, rejection rate, overrides, delinquency, and revenue generation, for example.
   - What is the model's validation frequency?
   - How reliable is vendor support?

Problem Credit Administration

3. Determine whether there is a centralized unit that administers problem credits.

4. Assess the criteria for loans managed by the centralized problem credit ("work-out") unit.

5. Determine whether assets managed by the problem credit unit are reflected in the risk rating stratification of the originating unit. This is to assure that concentrations of risk are adequately identified.

6. Determine whether losses are charged to the originating unit. This provides a more accurate measure of profitability, reinforces risk/reward analysis, and emphasizes officer accountability.

7. Evaluate the staff of the work-out function. Consider:

   • Number of staff and average account load.
   • Expertise and experience.
   • Access to external professionals.

8. How are work-out strategies devised? Do work-out strategies have clearly defined goals, benchmarks, and target dates? Are the financial benefits and costs of alternative strategies evaluated?

9. Review work-out MIS to determine whether sufficient information is provided to supervise work-out assets and monitor work-out strategies. Consider:

   • Rating changes of work-out assets.
   • Migration reports (assets coming in and going out).
   • Charge-off volumes.
   • Tracking reports to monitor the progress of work-out strategies.

10. Review the process for restructuring debt of troubled borrowers. Evaluate the oversight provided by the bank's accounting, legal, and audit departments.

Collections

10.   Determine whether there is a centralized collection unit.

11.   Evaluate the collection unit. Consider:

- Collection rate.
- Cost per dollar collected.
- Collection success by portfolio segment.
- Collection strategies.
- Use of technology.
- Collection MIS, including the following information:
  - collection rate reporting.
  - restructured loan levels and performance.
  - charge-off volumes.
  - quality of assets in collection.
- Productivity reports.
- Compliance with laws and regulations.

12.   Determine whether there are portfolios or credits being collected
       outside the collections area. If so, assess the reasons and ensure that
       controls are adequate. Analyze the agreement between the bank and
       the agency. Consider:

- Duties and responsibilities.
- Reporting requirements.
- Compensation levels and expenses compared with in-house
  departments.
- Complaints made against the agency.
- Whether the collection agency was selected in a competitive
  process.
- Whether there is a termination clause.

13.   Assess the policy for re-aging past-due credits. Evaluate the accounting
       practices used to report re-aged past due credits.

Charged-Off Assets

14. Evaluate management's analysis of charge-offs to determine their causes (the "post mortem" analysis). If no such analysis is conducted, determine whether credit risk management would be materially improved by doing so.

Allowance for Loan and Lease Losses

15. Confer with the examiner analyzing the allowance for loan and lease losses (ALLL).

- Determine that risk ratings are accurately reflected in bank management's ALLL analysis.
- Verify that ALLL loss projections are reasonable.
- Coordinate conclusions regarding quantity of risk and the direction of credit risk with the ALLL examiner.
- Determine whether credit risk is affected by the current ALLL level or by plans to materially change the level of the ALLL.

Portfolio Composition

1. Evaluate management's process for identifying loan concentrations within the portfolio.

- Are concentrations defined in terms of earnings, capital at risk, or both?
- Is the definition of a concentration reasonable? Is it an adequate safeguard for capital?
- Is the definition of a concentration sufficiently broad in light of the size and complexity of the bank's loan portfolio (ensure that the definition is not so narrow as to preclude any concentrations from being identified)?
- Can an asset be included in more than one concentration pool?
- What concentrations have been identified? How much capital supports them and, if management measures concentrations differently, how large are they when measured that way?

2. Are loan concentrations subject to close management attention?

    - Have limits on concentrations been set? If so, are they reasonable?
    - Review policy, underwriting, and documentation exceptions in identified concentrations. Evaluate the adequacy of exception tracking for concentration pools.
    - Have key financial indicators for each concentration been identified? If so, are they routinely monitored?

3. Compare the ratio of the largest relationships to total portfolio outstandings. Assess the changes to this ratio over time in order to determine whether management is permitting larger relationships. What are the implications for credit risk of these larger relationships and is management supervising these relationships more intensely?

4. Evaluate the policy to limit credit exposures. Confirm that the process used to limit credit exposures includes the following characteristics:

    - Relationship risk ratings.
    - Geography.
    - Product type.
    - Maturity.
    - Collateral.
    - Industry.
    - House or legal lending limit.

5. Ensure that all credit risk exposures (off-balance-sheet activity, contingent liability, related debt, etc.) are captured and included in the borrower's relationship for credit risk management purposes.

6. Determine whether management has developed portfolio diversification targets. If so, what are they?

7. Assess the integration of the bank's asset distribution targets into its overall risk management program or philosophy.

8. Verify the coordination of objectives and goals between asset distribution targets and the business/strategic plan.

9.   If portfolio composition has changed because of loan or portfolio acquisitions or sales:

● Determine the extent and adequacy of due diligence efforts.
● Evaluate the management process for making the decision to purchase or sell the assets.

10.   If the bank has an ongoing program to purchase loans, evaluate the credit risk in this program. Consider:

● Third-party underwriting standards,
● Recourse,
● Lending limit implications,
● Bank review of third-party paper,
● The bank's ability to reject loans under this program,
● Financial capacity of third party,
● Backroom support,
● Termination clauses,
● Legal, accounting, and loan review analysis of program.

11.   Can credit MIS identify and segregate assets purchased and underwritten outside the bank?

12.   Is the performance of acquired assets monitored as a separate loan pool? If so, how have the acquired assets performed? If there is no tracking system for acquired assets, a sample may have to be reviewed.

13.   Evaluate the loan portfolio management process for interest rate risk and liquidity factors.   Consider:

● Loan data and ALCO reporting requirements,
● Loan pricing decisions and cost of funds,
● Loan portfolio interest rate sensitivity,
● Cash flow from the portfolio,
● Portfolio maturity distribution, and
● Loan liquidity (quality, sale eligible, etc.).

14. Verify and evaluate management's assessment of risk when it set loan portfolio goals. Determine the appropriateness of the plan's goals to the risk assessment.

Personnel

1. Compare overall staffing levels in the lending and loan control areas with the size, complexity, and level of risk of the loan portfolio. Determine whether staffing levels will support planned or unplanned increases in any of these characteristics. Evaluate current management depth to determine its adequacy to support future growth objectives.

2. Determine whether a bank program ensures that staff acquires and retains the appropriate skills. If a training program exists, evaluate it. Consider:

   • Breadth and number of course offerings.
   • Structure of programs.
   • Course content and quality of instructors.
   • Measurement of students' understanding of material (testing).
   • Course materials.
   • Training commitment (dollars or hours per year) per employee.

3. Analyze the lending area's compensation plan and performance evaluation system.

   • Are asset-quality considerations in a proper balance with marketing considerations? Are performance criteria measurable?
   • How does the compensation of lending personnel compare with that of competitors?
   • How consistent are the compensation plan, performance evaluation system, the business/strategic plan, and the credit culture?

4. Evaluate whether reporting lines encourage open communication and limit the chances of conflicts of interest.

5. Determine whether the span of control for lending management is reasonable.

6. Assess the average account load per lending officer. Consider reasonableness in light of the complexity and condition of the officer's portfolio.

7. Evaluate the level of staff turnover and its impact on credit risk management.

8. Evaluate the process by which the quality of an account officer's portfolio is incorporated into his or her compensation and performance evaluation.

9. Interview bank personnel to determine whether they understand the bank's credit culture.

10. Determine whether the stated credit culture is reflected in the bank's goals, objectives, philosophy, and in the portfolio's composition. If not:

    • Describe the actual culture and evaluate the impact on risk in the portfolio.
    • Determine whether the difference between the stated credit culture and the actual credit culture results from lack of communication, management's indifference towards the stated culture, or a performance management system that rewards behaviors that are inconsistent with the stated credit culture.

11. Assess how senior management and the board of directors periodically evaluate bank personnel's understanding of and conformance with the bank's stated credit culture and loan policy. If there is no process, determine the impact on the management of credit risk.

Control Systems

1. Evaluate the adequacy of credit MIS. All evaluations of MIS should assess timeliness, accuracy, level of detail, clarity of report format, and distribution channels. Consider:

    *   Earnings and capital-at-risk measurements.
    *   Past-due and accrual status.
    *   Risk rating stratification.
    *   Loan yield and profitability data (per asset and portfolio).
    *   Trend analysis.
    *   Commitments, including type, amount, level of expected usage, and highest usage on record.
    *   Maturity categories.
    *   Liquidity information on loans and portfolios to include data on quality, maturity, and pledged collateral.
    *   Exceptions to policy, underwriting, and documentation standards.

2. Does management conduct a periodic review and evaluation of MIS and other internal controls? Is this evaluation frequent enough considering the sophistication of the control systems and the level of risk?

3. Review credit MIS and determine whether it provides sufficient detail about individual transactions, portfolio segments, and the entire portfolio.

4. Perform necessary testing to determine the accuracy of credit MIS. (If internal lending controls are satisfactory, testing for accuracy may be unnecessary.)

5. Evaluate the flexibility of the credit MIS system.

    *   Evaluate the distribution of credit MIS.
    *   Assess the amount and suitability of information provided to each layer of management.
    *   Evaluate credit MIS timeliness.

- Are the reports generated off a database that allows data manipulation? Can information be reported a number of ways (for example, by industry, product, and industry per product)?
- Can management design its own reports so it can access the type of information it wants?
- Can reports be developed quickly to respond to a specific need?
- Discuss with users whether adequate resources are devoted to MIS so information does not bottleneck.

6. If the bank conducts stress testing for credit risk, assess the following:

- The appropriateness of assumptions used in the stress test scenarios (for example, occupancy levels, raw material cost increases, and reduction in revenue growth).
- The amount of change each factor was subjected to.
- The financial measurements being tested (debt service coverage, leverage). Determine why management selected these measurements.
- What is stress tested — individual relationships, portfolio segments, the entire portfolio, or a combination of the foregoing?
- The frequency of credit stress testing in light of the portfolio's complexity and quality.
- The process for selecting loans or segments for stress testing. Is the selection process based on risk?
- How management uses stress test results. Have "acceptable" ranges been defined? If results exceed the "acceptable" range, is corrective action required?

7. Does stress testing incorporate all exposures (including off-balance-sheet exposure) to credit risk for each relationship?

8. Review the bank's risk rating definitions for consistency with regulatory definitions. If the definitions differ, determine whether the bank's ratings are adequate.

- Ensure that, when combining bank ratings with examiner ratings (to calculate the total risk rating stratification), definitions are similar enough to make the combination valid.

9. Evaluate the process for reviewing account officer risk ratings. Consider:

- Independence.
- Technical knowledge.
- Resources.
- Rating disagreement resolution process.

10. How often are relationships analyzed for risk rating purposes? Are there well-defined events that would require a risk rating analysis?

11. Evaluate risk rating analyses. Consider:

- Rating change triggers.
- Focus of analysis. (Are the appropriate credit risks and factors analyzed?)
- Relationship strategy.

12. Does an independent party analyze relationships frequently and thoroughly?

13. Assess the adequacy of loan review and loan-related audit reports. Consider:

- Whether all pertinent issues are brought forward in the report.
- Timeliness of report issuance.
- Clear assignment and acknowledgment of issue "ownership."
- Reasonableness and completeness of management responses. Is the issue addressed?
- Are there time limits on corrective action? Are the limits reasonable? Are they observed?
- How corrective actions are monitored and assessed.
- Do the reports contain enough information to inform senior management and the board about the condition of the portfolio and the effectiveness of internal controls?

14. If any control functions are performed by independent consultants (i.e., outsourced), review and evaluate the terms of the agreement. Consider:

   - Whether responsibilities are clearly defined.
   - Access to information.
   - Reporting lines.
   - How the consultant is paid.
   - Whether the agreement contains a termination clause.
   - How the consultant's conclusions are presented. How does the bank act on the consultant's recommendations?

15. Determine whether control function (loan review, audit, and "backroom") budgets and overall resources have kept pace with the changes in the loan portfolio.

16. Determine whether any audit or loan reviews have been postponed or canceled. If so, determine why. Verify that reviews were not delayed to avoid criticism. Determine whether the distribution of any audit or loan review reports has been delayed. If so, determine why.

17. Ensure that loan review is meeting its schedule and determine whether loan-related audits have been conducted as planned. If either are materially behind schedule determine the cause.

18. Determine whether control functions are independent. Consider:

   - Reporting lines.
   - Budget oversight.
   - Performance evaluation.
   - Compensation plans.
   - Access to the board.

19. Review the structure, charter, and mission of board and management credit committees.

   - Is the committee mission clear and well-defined?
   - Evaluate the committees' role in providing effective oversight.

- Assess the adequacy of information provided to the committees.
- Assess committee members attendance at meetings.

20. Has the board or senior management established adequate procedures for ensuring compliance with applicable laws and regulations?

21. Is the bank's internal control system appropriate for the type and level of risks undertaken within the loan portfolio?

Conclusion Procedures

Objective: To communicate findings and initiate corrective action when policies, practices, procedures, objectives, or internal controls are deficient or when violations of law, rulings, or regulations occur.

For banks with an asset quality component rating of "1" or "2":

1. Prepare a summary memorandum detailing the results of the loan portfolio management examination. Draft conclusions on:

   - The quantity of credit risk.
   - The quality of credit risk management.

2. Also address in the summary memorandum:
   - The direction of risk in the portfolio.
   - The extent to which credit risk management practices affect aggregate risk.
   - Appropriateness of strategic and business plans.
   - Adequacy and adherence to policies and underwriting standards.
   - Adequacy of MIS.
   - Compliance with applicable laws, rules, and regulations.
   - Adequacy of loan control functions.
   - Recommended corrective action regarding deficient policies, procedures, practices, or other concerns.
   - The bank's prospects.
   - Other matters of significance.

3. Assign appropriate CAMELS rating. The asset quality rating should incorporate the conclusions for quantity of risk and quality of risk management. Provide input to EIC for "M" component.

4. Discuss examination findings and conclusions with the EIC. If necessary, compose "Matters Requiring Board Attention" (MRBA) for the loan portfolio management examination. MRBAs should cover practices that:

- Deviate from sound, fundamental principles and are likely to result in financial deterioration if not addressed.
- Result in substantive noncompliance with laws.

MRBAs should discuss:

- Causes of the problem.
- Consequences of inaction.
- Management's commitment for corrective action.
- The time frame for corrective action and person(s) responsible for meeting that time frame.

5.   Discuss findings with bank management including conclusions about risks. If necessary, obtain commitments for corrective action.

6.   Write a memorandum specifically setting out what the OCC should do in the future to effectively supervise loan portfolio management. Include time frames, staffing, and workdays required.

7.   Update the supervisory record and any applicable report of examination schedules or tables.

8.   Update the examination work papers in accordance with OCC guidance.

For banks with an asset quality component rating of "3" or worse, perform the same steps as for banks rated "1" or "2." Then draw a conclusion regarding management's ability to correct the bank's fundamental weakness(es).

Topics of Loan Policy

The elements of a loan policy are determined by the specific lending activities and standards of each bank. However, most loan policies discuss the topics below.

- Loan Authority: The lending policy should describe who is authorized to approve credit and should establish specific approval limits for credit approvers. Lending limits may also be set for a group, allowing a combination of officers or a committee to approve loans larger than the members would be permitted to approve individually. Group approval may include dual controls: one approver from the line business unit and another from credit policy or a different line unit. The policy should describe reporting procedures and the frequency of committee meetings. Loan approval systems need to have sufficient flexibility to respond to unanticipated needs while maintaining adequate controls to prevent unwarranted risk.

- Limit on Aggregate Loans and Commitments: The loan policy may establish guidelines on the size of the loan portfolio relative to other balance sheet accounts (some banks will cover this topic in the ALCO policy). Limits should be developed for the aggregate volume of outstanding loans as well as for total commitments. A bank will find it much easier to develop a commitment limit if it has historical data on usage of its commitments during various phases of the credit cycle.

  Traditionally, limits have been set relative to deposits, capital, or total assets. As risk management is adopted more widely, banks are also developing limits on an activity's risk to earnings, capital, or both. A benefit of this approach is that limits are more closely tied to risk. The credit demands of the community, the volatility of the bank's funding, and the relative level of risk in the loan portfolio should also be considered when limiting the size of the loan portfolio.

- Distribution by Loan Category and Product: Policies also establish guidelines on the percentage of total loans that can be allocated to a particular loan category or concentration (e.g., commercial, real estate, consumer, international, and health care). Limits may also be placed on individual loan products within a loan category. For example, although a bank may already limit consumer loans in general, it can also limit installment loans or credit card loans. Loan category and product limits enable a bank to direct the composition of its loan portfolio to achieve strategic objectives rather than deferring to the demands of its market.

- Geographic Limits: The bank's geographic market should be identified, including any exceptions or specific restrictions. Geographic limits are consistent with the objective of serving the credit needs of the bank's community. They also help to ensure that the lending staff can supervise the loan portfolio effectively. Such supervision is especially important for new banks.

- Types of Loans: The lending policy may identify specific types of loans that the bank views as desirable or undesirable. For example, many banks do not finance business start-ups, and others avoid loans to gambling concerns. These guidelines should be based on the expertise of the lending staff, anticipated credit demands of the community, and the deposit structure of the bank. Real estate and other types of term lending, for example, might be limited to a given percentage of the bank's stable funds.

  Sophisticated credits and loans secured by collateral that requires inordinate policing should be avoided unless the bank has the personnel and resources to properly analyze and administer them. The lending policy can be used to control or avoid specific types of loans that have resulted in abnormal losses to the bank or that the bank considers undesirable.

- Financial performance standards: Financial performance standards usually are based on the purpose and type of loan. At a minimum, the policy should establish repayment requirements that stipulate acceptable primary and secondary sources of repayment, their relative adequacy, and circumstances in which guarantors are required. The policy may also require a certain minimum working capital, customer size, external agency credit rating, access to financial markets, leverage, and debt service coverage ratio.

- Financial information: Standards should stipulate what types of financial information are required and how frequently they are to be provided. The lending policy should define the financial statement requirements for businesses and individuals at various borrowing levels and set guidelines for audited, unaudited, fiscal, interim, operating, cash flow, guarantor, projections, and other types of statements. For example, audited financial statements might be required annually on all borrowers whose loans are greater than a certain amount.

  The policy should outline requirements for external credit checks. When external credit reporting agencies are used to determine the creditworthiness of borrowers, the information should be updated periodically. This is especially important for revolving consumer credit.

  Examiner guidance on citing credit exceptions in the report of examination is provided in appendix B of this section.

- Collateral and structure requirements: Policies usually describe acceptable credit structures and establish permissible collateral types and loan-to-value limits. They also establish limits for the amount financed, which may vary by loan type. For instance, the policy might limit loans to finance the purchase of equipment to 80 percent of purchase price and might limit the amortization schedule of such loans to the lesser of five years or the useful life of the equipment.

  Maturity scheduling should be based on a realistic assessment of the anticipated source of repayment, the purpose of the loan, and the useful life of the collateral. For term loans, the lending policy should define the maximum amortization period. Specific procedures may be needed when balloon payments are involved. Guidelines should be established for lines of credit, including the cleanup (out-of-debt) period and renewal requirements.

- Maximum Ratio of Loan Amount to the Market Value of Pledged Securities:
  In addition to the legal restrictions imposed by Regulation U (12 CFR 221), the lending policy should establish margin requirements for all types of securities accepted as collateral. Margin requirements should be related to the marketability of the security, i.e., whether it is actively traded, over-the-counter, or closely held. Guidelines should be developed for securities that periodically reprice. The bank should consider placing limits, modified margin requirements, or both on concentrations of loans to one industry or one borrower. Such concentrations occur most often in community banks located in an area dependent on one large company.

- Pricing Guidelines: Policies generally describe loan pricing principles. Interest rates and fees should be set at a level that covers the bank's cost of funds and overhead, and provides the bank with an acceptable return. In setting profit goals, management should consider the risk/reward relationship.

  Many banks use simplified pricing models or profitability analysis when granting credit to ensure uniform pricing by lenders. The information used in these models should be accurate and assumptions should be realistic. Banks may also use pricing to implement their strategic credit goals or to modify their risk profiles. Rates and fees may be set at levels that either encourage or discourage specific lines of business, certain industries, or certain types of customers. Pricing is one of the most effective ways that a bank can control or change its risk profile.

- Documentation Standards: Policies should establish guidelines for the internal and legal documents on various types loans. Internal documents include such items as borrowing resolutions, credit memoranda, financial analysis, appraisals, insurance, and processing documents; common legal documents are mortgages, security agreements, and UCC filings.

- Collections and Charge-Offs: The lending policy should require a systematic collection process that grows more aggressive as the risk of loss increases. Guidelines should specify charge-off requirements.

- Reporting: The lending policy may describe the types, contents, and frequency of reports provided to senior management and the board of directors. Common management reports include summaries of the level and trends of loans that are delinquent, nonaccrual, nonperforming, or charged off. It should also include reports on portfolio composition such as concentrations and policy exceptions. Reports on larger problem credits should include information on the level of risk, loss potential, and alternative courses of action.

- Limits and Guidelines for Loan Participations : Loan participations involve the sale and purchase of a portion of a loan or the whole loan. A participation certificate issued by the lead bank usually sets forth a purchaser's interest in the loan and in any collateral as well as the terms of the participation. The loan policy should be clear on how all transfer obligations are to be met.

  If sufficient loan demand exists, direct lending within the bank's trade area is generally safer and more profitable than purchasing loans. Direct lending promotes customer relationships, fosters the local economy, and helps to develop additional business for the bank. At the same time, purchasing loans can benefit risk management. Purchased loans can be a source of portfolio diversification, help balance interest rate gaps, be a source of liquidity if such loans can be easily resold, and help achieve strategic goals for particular loan products if a certain amount of such loans are necessary to meet economies of scale thresholds. For smaller banks, participations are an effective way to meet the credit needs of their customers while complying with the legal lending limit. Loan sales afford banks many of the benefits of loan participations.

  The lending policy may establish limits on the amount of loans that can be purchased from a single outside source and establish an aggregate limit for all purchased loans. The administration of purchased loans should be governed by the same credit principles and procedures that govern bank-originated loans. Supervisory standards and related regulatory requirements for loan participations are discussed in detail in appendix E.

- Off-Balance-Sheet Exposure: With the increase in bank securitization activity and the proliferation of capital markets products, more and more credit risk is housed off the balance sheet. Traditionally, off-balance-sheet credit risk has come primarily from loan commitments and letters of credit. The credit risk in these products is fairly straightforward, albeit there is always a measure of uncertainty about whether the facility will be drawn. The credit risk inherent in the capital markets products is more difficult to quantify because of the need to assign a credit risk equivalent. As for securitizations, the bank's residual exposure to the sold assets is also difficult to measure. (The booklet "Asset Securitization" provides guidance on credit risk associated with securitizations.) The loan policy should require that off-balance-sheet and any other indirect exposure is included in exposure limits and subject to periodic review and renewal as part of the loan approval process.

- Other Matters: A bank can supplement its general lending policy with guidelines and procedures for specific lending departments. Other lending-related booklets of the Comptroller's Handbook focus on loan policy for specific types of lending.

12 CFR 30 — Safety and Soundness Standards

Guidelines for Loan Documentation Practices

Appendix A (II,C) to 12 CFR 30, Interagency Guidelines Establishing Standards for Safety and Soundness, provides that a bank should establish and maintain loan documentation practices that:

- Enable the bank to make an informed lending decision and to assess risk, as necessary, on an ongoing basis.

- Identify the purpose of a loan and the source of repayment, and assess the ability of the borrower to repay the indebtedness in a timely manner.

- Ensure that any claim against a borrower is legally enforceable.

- Demonstrate appropriate administration and monitoring of a loan.

- Take account of the size and complexity of a loan.

Guidelines for Credit Underwriting Practices

Appendix A(II,D) to part 30 also provides that a bank should establish and maintain prudent credit underwriting practices that:

- Are commensurate with the types of loans the bank will make and consider the terms and conditions under which they will be made.

- Consider the nature of the markets in which loans will be made.

- Provide for consideration, before making a credit commitment, of the borrower's overall financial condition and resources, the financial responsibility of any guarantor, the nature and value of any underlying collateral, and the borrower's character and willingness to repay as agreed.

- Establish a system of independent, ongoing credit review and appropriate communication to management and to the board of directors.

- Take adequate account of concentration of credit risk.

- Are appropriate to the size of the bank and the nature and scope of its activities.

Portfolio Credit Risk Management Processes

OCC Advisory Letter 97-3 describes nine elements of an effective portfolio credit risk management process. Those elements are described below.

Assessment of the Credit Culture

A bank's credit culture, which is the sum of its values, beliefs, and behaviors, should reflect the standards and values of the board of directors and senior management. Every bank has a credit culture, whether articulated or implied. Banks that perform well consistently have a credit culture that is clearly understood throughout the organization. Senior management and the board should periodically assess whether employees' understanding of the bank's credit culture, and their resulting behavior, conform with the desired standards and values for the bank. Independent audit and internal loan review functions can help in this assessment.

Because the credit culture influences every aspect of the credit process, including credit risk selection and underwriting, a bank's sales strategies must be coordinated with its credit risk management objectives. In addition, compensation systems for the lending area should reward the kind of behavior that is consistent with long-term credit quality objectives.

Portfolio Objectives and Risk Tolerance Limits

For portfolio management to be effective, management should establish and clearly communicate the bank's strategic objectives. The bank also should consider identifying objectives for every key portfolio segment. A business plan to achieve these objectives should be a part of, and consistent with, the bank's overall planning process.

Management should use those objectives to establish risk tolerance limits. As those limits are approached, the risk management process should require that the board of directors and/or senior management review the portfolio to assess the reasons for the increased level of risk and to take appropriate action. Management should periodically evaluate each lending unit's business and marketing plan for consistency with strategic portfolio objectives.

Effective risk management also should include a periodic review of lending policies and underwriting criteria. Before implementing any proposed changes to policies or standards, management should estimate their potential effect on risk tolerance limits, the bank's overall risk profile, and the bank's ability to meet its portfolio objectives. Those estimates should later be tested by comparing them with actual experience.

Management Information Systems

Effective portfolio credit risk management depends on adequate management information systems (MIS). Industry consolidation and the relatively long expansionary phase of the lending cycle have provided some banks with the opportunity to increase their loan portfolios significantly, often by entering new' markets and product areas. However, the OCC has observed that the credit MIS capabilities of some banks have not kept pace with this growth. The OCC encourages bank senior management and board members to assess periodically the adequacy of their bank's credit MIS in light of recent loan growth, acquisitions, and changes in the bank's appetite for risk. The maintenance of an adequate credit MIS gives banks the ability to segment their loan portfolios and to assess risks more accurately.

Portfolio Segmentation and Risk Diversification Objectives

The selection and management of individual credit transactions remains an important part of managing a bank's credit risk, but portfolio credit risk management also involves looking at entire segments of the portfolio — groups of loans with similar risk characteristics. Bank management may make a different decision about underwriting requirements for an individual transaction if it takes into account the risk profile of the bank's entire portfolio rather than focusing only on the individual transaction.

Effective portfolio management requires an understanding of all of the risk characteristics of the portfolio. A bank should segment its portfolio in a number of different ways — for example, by loan type, industry, geography, structure, collateral, tenor, and risk of default or loss. The same loan may be included in several portfolio segments based on different risk elements.

Risk diversification is fundamental to portfolio management. The bank should identify the risk characteristics of each segment. And, as part of concentration management, the bank also should try to identify possible covariances, similarities, or interrelationships among portfolio segments. Identifying these shared risks is critical in developing diversification strategies.

Analysis of Loans Originated by Other Lenders

Another part of portfolio credit risk management is assessing the effect of loans originated and underwritten at other financial institutions on a bank's credit risk profile. These loans include individual syndicated credits and participations and loans acquired through portfolio purchases. The OCC is concerned that some downstream participants may be purchasing loans based on underwriting standards significantly different from their own. The acquisition of any such credits should be subject to proper due diligence.

The OCC encourages banks to consider the credit risks associated with syndicated credits and participations from the perspective of overall portfolio management. Before participating in a syndication or participation, a bank should evaluate the risk of the proposed credit to determine whether the loan is consistent with its portfolio strategy and risk tolerance. Because these decisions often have a short deadline, an effective portfolio management process is essential. Bankers should not invest in such credits without a thorough understanding of their bank's risk acceptance criteria and the portfolio risk consequences.

The same portfolio risk concepts apply to the purchase of entire portfolios. A bank must conduct sufficient due diligence to understand fully the credit risks that it would assume in the purchase of a portfolio. The portfolio should be appropriately segmented, and the credit risk should be properly evaluated. Any decision to purchase, including the price at which to purchase, should take into account the effect the loans will have on the bank's overall portfolio risk profile.

Banking Circular No. 181 (Revised), dated August 2, 1984, provides further guidance regarding the purchase of loans and highlights actions required to document, analyze, and control credit risk on such loans.

Aggregate Policy and Underwriting Exception System

Every bank should have a process to identify and approve loan policy and underwriting exceptions and to document any mitigating factors. Most banks do have effective systems for approving and monitoring exceptions for individual transactions. However, just as the best way for a bank to understand the full extent of its credit risk is to analyze aggregate loan data, an important part of analyzing exceptions is to track and analyze policy and underwriting exceptions in the aggregate.

Portfolio credit risk management is facilitated by reporting systems that capture and track information on exceptions, both by transaction and by relevant portfolio segments. The aggregate data is useful in assessing portfolio risk profiles, reassessing existing policy and standards, and evaluating the adequacy of the allowance for loan and lease losses. The data also may serve as an oversight tool for monitoring the level of adherence to policy and underwriting standards by departments or individual lenders. A bank's analysis of the information also may reveal a correlation between certain types of exceptions and migration of internal risk ratings.

Stress Testing for Portfolios

In addition to stress testing significant individual credits, bank management should consider developing "what if" scenarios for key portfolio segments. The scenarios would identify possible credit risk triggers or events that could increase risk for a portfolio segment or for the portfolio as a whole. The trigger events may include interest rate changes, commodity or other price shocks, economic cycles, or technological, political, or sociological changes. Using scenarios can be more helpful if several possibilities are considered and probabilities are assigned to each. One good, basic approach is to develop best, worst, and most likely scenarios for each portfolio segment and then to project the outcomes.

Bank management should also consider developing contingency plans for scenarios and outcomes that involve credit risk in excess of the bank's established risk tolerances. These plans might include increasing monitoring, limiting portfolio growth, and possibly hedging or exit strategies for both significant individual transactions and key portfolio segments.

Independent and Effective Control Functions

Management should have control systems to ensure that credit extensions are consistent with strategic portfolio and risk objectives. Reliable identification, measurement, and monitoring of portfolio credit risk is possible only if control systems ensure the accuracy of information. There are many control functions throughout the lending process; in most banks, the key control functions are loan review and audit.

The board of directors and senior management should ensure that these important control functions are independent of the lending function and are staffed adequately to perform their assigned duties. As bank systems and composition of the portfolio become more sophisticated, the bank should ensure that the expertise and experience of staff in the loan review and audit functions keep pace. A bank should not attempt to achieve its operating objectives at the expense of these necessary control functions.

Analysis of Portfolio Risk/reward Tradeoffs

Portfolio credit risk management is not sufficient if it does not take into account the bank's range of acceptable risk/reward relationships. The OCC encourages banks to research and experiment with risk pricing models. The models should consider individual transactions; relationship management, including risks and revenues from all sources; and portfolio segment risk/reward.

Loan Production Offices

Many national banks have established loan production offices to solicit and originate business outside their main offices and authorized branches. The solicitation and origination of loans by bank employees at loan production offices (LPOs) is governed by Interpretive Ruling 7.1004, which requires that the loans be approved and made at the main office or a branch office of the bank or at an office of the LPO located on the premises of, or contiguous to, the main office or a branch office of the bank.

Interpretive Ruling 7.1004 lists the following activities as examples of what can be done at any LPO, regardless of location:

- Soliciting loan business using, for example, advertisements disclosing the nature and limitations of the loan production office.

- Providing information on loan rates and terms.

- Interviewing and counseling applicants regarding loans, including giving them disclosures required by regulations such as Regulation Z of the Federal Reserve Board.

Examiners should be alert for two practices that the interpretive ruling does not allow. The first practice is originating and approving loans at a loan production office, while disbursing funds from a main office or a branch. Disbursing funds from the main office or a branch does not satisfy the interpretive ruling since the loans are approved at the loan production office.

The second practice is making lending decisions at the LPO and forwarding loans from the LPO to the main office or a branch for perfunctory approval and disbursement. The interpretive ruling requires that bank employees at the main office or a branch approve loans in accordance with safe and sound banking practices by reviewing the credit quality of the loans and determining that they meet the bank's credit standards. Although employees at the main office or a branch may consider recommendations made by the loan production office when assessing the credit quality of a loan, they must make independent, considered decisions.

Loan Participations

A participation, as distinguished from a multi-bank loan transaction (syndicated loan), is an arrangement in which a bank makes a loan to a borrower and then sells all or a portion of that loan to another bank. All documentation is drafted in the name of the selling bank. Generally, the purchasing bank's share of the participated loan is evidenced by a certificate that assigns an interest in the loan and any related collateral.

The purchase and sale of loans and participations in loans are established banking practices. Such transactions serve legitimate needs of the buying and selling banks and the public interest. However, the absence of satisfactory controls over risk may constitute an unsafe or unsound banking practice.

Satisfactory controls over the purchase of loans and participations in loans ordinarily include, but are not limited to, the following:

- Sound policies and procedures governing these transactions.

- An independent analysis of credit quality by the purchasing bank.

- Agreement by the obligor to make full credit information available to the selling bank.

- Agreement by the selling bank to provide available information on the obligor to the purchaser.

- Written documentation of recourse arrangements outlining the rights and obligations of each party.

Policy and Procedures

The purchase of loans, loan participations, and loan portfolios should be governed by the credit principles and procedures contained in the purchasing bank's formal lending policy. The policy ordinarily should require:

- Complete analysis and documentation of the credit quality of obligations to be purchased.

- An analysis of the value and lien status of the collateral.

- The maintenance of full credit information on the obligor during the term of the loan.

Independent Credit Analysis

To make a prudent credit decision, the purchasing bank should conduct an independent credit analysis to satisfy itself that the loan, loan participation, or loan portfolio meets its internal credit standards. The nature and extent of this independent analysis should be based on the type of transaction being considered and the purchaser's lending policies and procedures. When loans are purchased in bulk, for example, a prudent purchaser might assess the credit of the class of obligors rather than each obligor.

Despite a favorable analysis of a loan by the seller, a credit rating institution, or another entity, the purchasing bank should conduct an independent credit analysis. A purchaser may, however, consider analyses obtained from the seller and other sources.

To make an informed and independent evaluation of a credit, a purchaser should have full credit information on an obligor. After the purchase is made, the purchaser also needs timely credit information to monitor the status of the credit. Although this information can often be obtained from the seller, sometimes the information is insufficient. If it is, the purchaser should look to other sources of information.

Prudent Transfer Agreements

The indirect relationship between the obligor and the purchaser makes it difficult for the purchaser to assess the quality of the loan without the cooperation of the selling or servicing bank. The purchaser ordinarily should obtain full credit information on the obligor from the selling or servicing bank at the outset and during the life of the participation. With such information at hand, the purchaser should perform a continuing independent assessment of the credit. Thus, the purchase or participation document should include an agreement by the selling or servicing bank to continually provide any available credit information on the obligor to the purchasing bank.

This is not intended to suggest that existing loan and participation agreements need to be renegotiated when full credit information is not being furnished. Nonetheless, the examiner should recommend appropriate action in any case when less than full credit information is obtained.

The absence of prudent transfer agreements may affect a purchaser's ability to obtain, assess, and maintain sufficient credit information. Accordingly, the purchase of a loan or participation in the absence of such transfer obligations may be viewed as an unsafe or unsound banking practice.

Scope of Prudent Transfers

Transferred credit information should be sufficient in scope to enable a purchaser to make an informed and independent credit decision. Full and timely financial information should be transferred, as well as any nonfinancial information that could help determine the quality of a loan. For example, any known changes in the obligor's corporate structure or management would generally be disclosed.

Note: References to "full" and "timely" transfers of credit information are intended to provide supervisory guidelines on safe and sound transfers of credit information. The guidelines describe the scope of transfers required for a purchaser to make an informed and independent credit decision. Apart from such supervisory considerations, use of the terms "full" and "timely" is not intended to suggest that the terms have particular legal significance; thus, other terms may be used. The drafting and negotiation of standards

---

governing transfers of credit information are the responsibility of bank management and counsel.

Financial information ordinarily includes:

- Accrual status.

- Status of principal and interest payments.

- Financial statements, collateral values, and lien status.

- Any factual information that affects the creditworthiness of the obligor.

Ordinarily, full credit information is obtained on each obligor. When loans are purchased in bulk, however, credit information on the class of obligors rather than each obligor could be sufficient for a prudent purchaser.

The selling bank should not release information if doing so would violate the law. In particular, loan classification information and other examiner opinions in confidential reports of examination and related documents may not be disclosed without the express written approval of the Comptroller of the Currency pursuant to 12 CFR 4.18(c). Unauthorized disclosures may incur criminal penalties under 18 USC 641. The facts underlying examiners' loan criticisms can generally be furnished. A knowing misrepresentation of credit quality may violate 18 USC 1014.

Recourse Arrangements

Repurchase agreements are subject to the limitations of 12 USC 84. If the selling bank makes any direct or indirect recourse arrangements, written or oral, that are not permitted by 12 USC 84, these arrangements are considered to be extensions of credit to the selling bank subject to 12 USC 84. See 12 CFR 32.2(j)(1)(iv) and (j)(2)(vi).

Prudent recourse arrangements are documented in writing and reflected on the books and records of both the buying and selling bank. The failure to properly record or document these arrangements may constitute a false entry, statement, report, or representation in violation of 18 USC 1005.

Sale and Purchase of U.S. Government-Guaranteed Loans

Examiners should review loan sale and purchase activities for government-guaranteed loans. Lax or improper management of a selling bank's servicing responsibilities should be criticized. Lending out of the trade area for the purpose of reselling any portion of U.S. government-guaranteed loans should be carefully reviewed to ensure that the practice is conducted in a safe and sound manner.

All income, including servicing fees and premiums charged in lieu of servicing fees, associated with the sale of U.S. government-guaranteed loans should be recognized as earned and amortized to appropriate income accounts over the life of the loan.

Banks purchasing U.S. government-guaranteed loans should be aware that the purchase premiums are not guaranteed and, if the loans are prepaid, are not paid by the guaranteeing federal agency. It is generally considered an unsafe and unsound banking practice for a bank to pay purchase premiums that result in the value of bank assets being significantly overstated. Payment of premiums that do not reasonably relate to the yield on a loan can distort published financial reports by overstating the value of a bank's assets.

Many variable-rate, government-guaranteed loans normally should not trade at anything more than a modest premium or discount. Examiners should carefully review any loans being sold or purchased at significant premiums and should criticize any transactions with excessive premiums as unsafe and unsound. Excessive purchase premiums should be classified loss. The loans should be revalued to the market value at the time of the acquisition and the excessive premiums charged against current earnings.

In addition, any unamortized loan premium on a government-guaranteed loan must be immediately charged against income if the loan is prepaid, regardless of whether payment is received from the borrower or the guaranteeing agency.

The guaranteed portions of U.S. government-guaranteed loans should not be recorded or carried as U.S. government or federal agency securities. They should be carried and reported as U.S. government-guaranteed loans.

Loan Brokerage and Servicing Activities

Banks are engaging in more and more off-balance-sheet activities, including the origination, sale, and servicing of various types of loans. Off-balance-sheet activity is common in mortgage lending and occurs increasingly in other consumer lending and in government-guaranteed lending (or portions thereof) and credit card lending. Selling banks can generate income from loan servicing fees and can reinvest the proceeds of the sales.

If loan sale proceeds are continually reinvested in new loan originations, the volume of servicing assets may pose a risk. While loan servicing operations usually benefit from economies of scale, the bank must recognize the increased level of operational risk and take steps to ensure that it does not become responsible for servicing more loans than it can effectively manage. Failure to administer the loans properly may lead to legal or financial liabilities that could severely affect bank capital. Examiners should review the extent and nature of servicing activities to ensure that they are conducted in a safe and sound manner. They should also ensure that servicing fees and premiums charged in lieu of fees are amortized over the life of the loan. Improper practices should be criticized.

Examiners should refer to the Comptroller's Handbook booklet on "Asset Securitization" for a more complete discussion of the risks associated with off-balance-sheet activities.

IRS Express Determination Letters

This appendix outlines the procedures for issuing an express determination letter in connection with the Internal Revenue Service (IRS) regulations relating to bank-initiated charge-offs. It supplements appendix C, "Certification Procedures for Consumer Loans Charged Off between Examinations" in the "Instalment Lending" booklet of the Comptroller's Handbook. The procedures contained in appendix C of "Instalment Lending" remain in effect for banks that choose not to operate under the new regulations.

Background

The IRS has issued regulations on the deductibility of loan charge-offs by financial institutions. Under these regulations, institutions may elect to put their tax accounting for bad debts in conformity with their regulatory accounting. Institutions electing to do so will automatically be allowed to deduct charge-offs of loss assets for federal income tax purposes in the same year the charge-offs are taken for regulatory purposes.

The regulations require an institution to maintain loan loss classification standards that are consistent with the standards established for loan charge-offs by its primary federal supervisory agency. If the institution meets these requirements, its loan charge-offs are conclusively presumed worthless for federal income tax purposes. These regulations are effective for taxable years ending on or after December 31, 1991.

Election Requirements

To be eligible, an institution must file a conformity election with its federal tax return. The IRS regulations also require the institution's primary federal supervisory agency to expressly determine whether the institution maintains and applies classification standards for loan charge-offs that are consistent with regulatory requirements.

Procedures

The bank is responsible for requesting an express determination letter during each examination that covers the loan review process.

When a bank that has made or intends to make the election under IRS Regulation 1.166-2(d)(3) requests such a letter, the examiner may issue one similar to the sample letter following this appendix, provided the bank maintains and applies loan loss classification standards that are consistent with regulatory requirements.

The letter should be issued only when an examination covering the bank's loan review process is completed and when the examiner has concluded that it is appropriate to issue it. Examiners should not alter the scope or frequency of examinations merely to permit a bank to use this regulation.

The letter should be signed and dated by the examiner-in-charge and given to the bank for its files. The letter is not part of the examination report. The examiner's conclusions on the bank's loan loss classification standards should appear in examination workpapers.

OCC standards for loan charge-offs and classification standards are set forth in this booklet's sections on instalment loans, credit card loans, and classification of credits.

The determination letter should be issued only when:

• The examination indicates that the bank maintains and applies loan loss classification standards that are consistent with OCC standards regarding the identification of losses and the charge-off of loans.

• There are no material deviations from regulatory standards.

Minor criticisms of the bank's loan review process or immaterial deviations from regulatory standards should not preclude issuance of the letter.

The letter should not be issued when:

- Examiners have significantly criticized the bank's loan review process on charge-offs.

- Loan charge-offs are consistently overstated or understated on call reports.

- The bank has a pattern of failing to recognize loan charge-offs in the appropriate year.

Revoking the Election

The bank's election of the new method is revoked automatically if the examiner does not issue an express determination letter following an examination covering the loan review process. The OCC is not required to rescind any previously issued express determination letters.

An examiner's decision to withhold the determination letter revokes the election for the current year. However, it does not invalidate a bank's election for any previous years. Withholding the determination letter places the burden of proof on the bank to support its tax deductions for loan charge-offs.

Sample Letter

Date

Chief Executive Officer
National Bank

EXPRESS DETERMINATION LETTER FOR IRS REGULATION 1.166-2(d)(3)

In connection with the most recent examination of [NAME OF BANK] by the Office of the Comptroller of the Currency, we reviewed the institution's loan review process as it relates to loan charge-offs.   Based on our review, we concluded that the bank, as of [EXAMINATION CLOSE DATE], maintained and applied loan loss classification standards that were consistent with regulatory standards regarding loan charge-offs.

This statement is made on the basis of a review that was conducted in accordance with our normal examination procedures and criteria, including sampling of loans in accordance with those procedures and criteria. It does not in any way limit or preclude any formal or informal supervisory action (including enforcement actions) by this supervisory authority relating to the institution's loan review process or the level at which it maintains its allowance for loan and lease losses.

Sincerely yours,

National Bank Examiner
Examiner-in-charge

Laws, Regulations, and Rulings

Banking Laws for Examiners, OCC
Banking Regulations for Examiners, Volumes 1 - 4, OCC
(See the subject index in the back of Banking Laws for the laws, regulations, or rulings sought.)

Interagency Policy Statements

Federal Financial Institutions Examination Council Supervisory Policy, "The Sale of U.S. Government-Guaranteed Loans and Sale Premiums,"
May 7, 1985
Interagency Policy Statement, "Allowance for Loan and Lease Losses,"
December 21, 1993
    Attachment 1, "Loan Review Systems"
    Attachment 2, "International Transfer Risk Considerations"

Accounting and Reporting Issues

Accounting Principles Board Opinion 21, "Interest on Receivables and Payables"
Bank Accounting Advisory Series, OCC, June 1994
FAS 15, "Accounting by Debtors and Creditors for Troubled Debt Restructurings"
FAS 66, "Accounting for Sales of Real Estate"
FAS 114, "Accounting by Creditors for Impairment of a Loan"
Federal Financial Institutions Examination Council, "Consolidated Reports of Condition and Income — Instructions"

www.ingramcontent.com/pod-product-compliance
Lightning Source LLC
Chambersburg PA
CBHW080313290526
45790CB00005B/2020